INTO THE HEART OF ADVENT

INTO THE HEART OF ADVENT

Twenty-five conversations with Jesus

Penelope Wilcock

First published in Great Britain in 2020

Society for Promoting Christian Knowledge
36 Causton Street
London SW1P 4ST
www.spck.org.uk

British Library Cataloguing-in-Publication Data
A catalogue record for this book is available from the British Library

ISBN 978–0–281–08443–2
eBook ISBN 978–0–281–08444–9

1 3 5 7 9 10 8 6 4 2

Typeset by Nord Compo
First printed in Great Britain by Jellyfish Print Solutions

eBook by Nord Compo

Produced on paper from sustainable forests

For

Michael and Iceni Garner
and for Andy Knight

Contents

Contents

Acknowledgements

Near the end of this book, in chapters twenty-one and twenty-two, there is some information about the circumstances surrounding the birth of Jesus that may or may not be familiar to you. This information is easy to research and verify in these days when search engines make the whole world our library, but I would like to acknowledge some sources through which the information came to me.

In 2018 an article was passed on to me, written by Elsa Henderson in 2014, and entitled *Shepherds of Bethlehem*. I know nothing more about Elsa, nor where her article was originally published, but I would like to credit her here with first introducing me to the Tower of the Flock, Migdal Eder, where Jesus was probably laid in the manger (see my Chapter Twenty-One, 'The manger'). If you do an internet search on The Tower of the Flock, you will have the opportunity to read a number of articles expanding on this interesting topic; but I heard it first from Elsa Henderson.

In respect of the season of the year when Jesus was born, again there is an abundance of information, opinion and explanation online, but I found particularly helpful an article entitled *The Season of Jesus' Birth – When?* and subtitled *Shepherding in the Land*, written by Hani Abu Dayyeh for the website Discover the Bible Lands. You can read it here: <http://www.discoverthebiblelands.com /the-season-of-jesus-birth-when-was-it/>

Then in Chapter Twenty-Two, 'Room at the inn', I have written about the misunderstandings surrounding Luke's gospel account that says Jesus was laid in a manger because there was no room at the inn. I first came across this information in an article written by Mario Seiglie and Tom Robinson, for the United Church of God website in 2012, entitled *Was there really 'No room in the inn'?* You can find it here online: <https://www.ucg.org/the-good-news/was-there-really-no-room-in-the-inn>

Again, if you do an internet search on the word *kataluma*, you will find numerous articles on this topic, but I first came across it in the article I have referenced above.

Since the electronic revolution, access to scholarly information has become easy and quick, but it should still be credited. I am grateful for Elsa Henderson, Hani Abu Dayyeh, Mario Seiglie and Tom Robinson, for giving me insights into the birth narratives of Jesus that made such very good sense.

Introduction

I believe imagination is the gateway into transformative understanding. You can't make change or develop spiritually without engaging the imagination. It projects ahead of you like Moses parting the sea, making a way through to the place you haven't got to yet. Then all you have to do is walk forward.

Imagination is kindled through stories. They make what is inchoate into something present and alive. They allow meaning to come home.

I have done my best to harness this process through thirty years of writing. I've written some straightforward pastoral theology, but in the main my endeavour has been in the area of what I think of as fusion literature – a mixture of equal parts theological exposition and fiction.

Usually in a work of fiction the reader is given a window into a world, watching the comings and goings while personally sitting outside. There will be responses, of course – mainly emotional – excitement of various kinds produced by the threat or the erotic content or the tension or character antagonisms and resolutions. The reader may 'lose herself' in the story, but does that not imply she and the story are two separate things? When she regains herself at the end, she is back out of the story; they are once more distinct and she leaves it behind.

In my fusion literature, what I've tried to write is *your story*, leaving a permanently open door through which you may come and go into the transformative world of the imagination.

I believe the scriptures are not a closed and finished canon; I believe the journey they indicate, the direction of travel, continues in the unfolding sacred scripture of your life. The purposes of God chronicled there have another chapter and another, in the continuing sequence of our everyday world. I've tried also to create a pathway both fictional and real (that's exactly what imagination is) along which readers can start to walk, then continue without a break into their personal context. I wrote a series of nine novels (*The Hawk & the Dove* stories), creating a community of the imagination into which the reader is welcomed as a member. The community abides as a transformative context incorporating everyday life; it offers a refuge where those who dip into it can strengthen and refresh discipleship on an ongoing basis, spinning their own stories from the ones I wrote.

I also wrote two volumes of short fiction pieces – *52 Original Wisdom Stories* (exploring the round of the ecclesiastical year and its connections with the old Celtic agricultural year), and a Lent book, *The Wilderness Within You* (exploring the possibility of what it might mean to give imaginative shape to the Christian discipline of spending time in the presence of Jesus every day, telling him what's in our hearts and listening for his guidance).

The book you're embarking on now continues in this vein. These chapters expand and reflect upon the teaching of the church and the scriptures, as I understand them, but also offer a template for taking the sacred narrative forward into everyday experience, intending that it may prove useful in your own discipleship practice as it is in mine.

I hope it will be at the very least a light breeze in your sails as you make your own voyage; your journey is your own and only you can make it, but borrowing imaginatively from one another's stories can help us chart our passage and lift our sails.

May your adventuring and exploring be blessed. May the story your life is writing have a happy ending. May the chapter you are living now be satisfying to you. May your imagination be kindled, and may your feet find the path into the meaning of things, the trustworthy way home.

1

The holy family

Then Jesus entered a house, and again a crowd gathered,
so that he and his disciples were not even able to eat.
When his family heard about this, they went to take charge of him,
for they said, 'He is out of his mind.'. . .
. . . A crowd was sitting round him, and they told him,
'Your mother and brothers are outside looking for you.'
'Who are my mother and my brothers?' he asked.
Then he looked at those seated in a circle round him and said,
'Here are my mother and my brothers! Whoever does God's will
is my brother and sister and mother.'
(Mark 3.20-21, 32-35 NIVUK)

I stand in the shop looking indecisively at the cards on display, slowly twirling the revolving rack. I've chosen the ones I like, with deer and robins and snow, but I think in all truth I ought to pick out at least a few showing the infant Jesus and his mother. Because that's what Christmas is all about, right? The nativity, and at the heart of it, the holy family. The problem is, I don't like them. Mary looks either demure or mournful, and the baby Jesus stares out reproachfully at our fallen world, raising two fingers in blessing like a miniature Boy Scout or the youngest member of an extremely secret society.

Someone is standing next to me. I glance over my shoulder, not wanting to put pressure upon the patience of another customer ticking off Christmas obligations early. And then I do a double take – 'Jesus! Where did you come from? I mean . . . Hello.' And just like that, there he is again. Himself, whom I haven't seen in ages.

'Stick with the robins,' he suggests. 'Those are awful.'

'But, shouldn't I have at least some nativity ones? Christmas – it's all about family, isn't it? Especially your family.'

'My family . . .' says Jesus. 'Look, shall we get out of this shop?'

I pay for the few packs I'm sure I want, shove them into my bag with the TV guide and the oranges, and hurry outside to find him. Then, just like old times, we stroll along the seafront in the wind.

'This unbreakable connection between family and Christmas comes back to haunt me every year,' I tell him. 'I'm divorced; I have a difficult relationship with my step-family, and my family of origin – ha! Don't even go there! There's nothing like Christmas to rub it all in, that all too familiar ambiance of utter despair. And there are the cards with you as a baby, cradled in Mary's arms while Joseph stands protectively beside her.'

Jesus says nothing for a moment, and I glance at him to see his reaction. He grins at me. 'Are you even thinking about what you're saying? My mother . . . reckless prophetess writing protest songs and trying to steer me into her idea of who I should be. My mother conscripting my brothers into getting me sectioned. Joseph thinking best to divorce her before they even began, and introducing his betrothed

2

to his relatives on the night she was due to drop an embar-
rassingly early baby. Awkward.'

I consider this in silence.

'If there's one useful takeaway from looking at my family,' he adds, 'it's that you just get the hand life deals you. It's
the part you can't plan, even if you try. Joseph chose cautiously, carefully; he well knew how important it is to find
a good wife. He was after a godly woman. But then he got a
really godly woman, and that shook his world. Dreams and
visions, angels and journeys, soldiers with swords in their
hands. He had no idea what he was taking on when he asked
Mary to be his wife.'

I stop, turn to face him, pulling my coat closer around me
because the wind is so cold. 'Then, what – if you could pick
out one thing – what would you say Christmas is all about?'

'Me? My point of view?' He looks at me. 'I'd say Christmas is about saying "yes". That's the one thing Mary and
Joseph and I all had in common. Mary said "yes" to the
angel, and Joseph – against his own inclination – said "yes"
to marrying Mary after all, and I said "yes" to . . . well, to
everything it meant as things unfolded. "Yes" to being here,
"yes" to pouring out all my strength to bring healing and
hope, "yes" to offering a template for living that's actually
going to work. We said "yes", and that was the thing that
brought us together.'

I nod, slowly, taking this in. 'That's what made you family – saying "yes"?'

Jesus is never impatient, but I do detect just a tad of frus-
tration in the movement of his hand. 'Can we get something
clear?' he says. 'My family is everyone who says "yes" to life

and love. My family isn't frozen in time back in Nazareth. Anyone who wants can join my family. *You* are my family, if you want to be. Just bear in mind, when you trace the way things went for Mary and Joseph and me, there is a cost. But isn't there always, to loving?'

2

Expectancy and expectations

Jesus began to speak to the crowd about John:
'What did you go out into the wilderness to see?
A reed swayed by the wind? If not, what did you go out to see?
A man dressed in fine clothes? No, those who wear expensive
clothes and indulge in luxury are in palaces.
But what did you go out to see? A prophet?
Yes, I tell you, and more than a prophet. This is the one
about whom it is written:
"I will send my messenger ahead of you,
who will prepare your way before you."
I tell you, among those born of women
there is no one greater than John; yet the one who is least
in the kingdom of God is greater than he.'
(Luke 7.24-28 NIVUK)

I like being with Jesus. I don't think you'd necessarily expect this, but his company is both comforting and relaxing. If I didn't know better, I'd have imagined his presence might make me nervous, in case I couldn't live up to his expectations of me; but, I *do* know better – he doesn't have any.

Just now, as we walk up the hill from the sea with the intention of putting the kettle on for a nice cup of tea, it feels so easy and natural walking along beside him. There's something about Jesus that takes the strain out of life. He doesn't have to say or do anything – just being alongside him brings me peace.

We walk in silence, but I'm turning over in my mind that Advent is a time of waiting. It correlates with the old Celtic 'No-Time', that strange season after the ending of the old year at All Hallows, and before the birth of new light at the winter solstice. In No-Time the days drift suspended between the old and the new, with nothing to belong to, just waiting. In Advent, we wait, but as always the church has managed to find itself at loggerheads with everyone else; because *we're* waiting for the second coming and searching our hearts in preparation for meeting Christ our Judge, while all around us everyone else is getting ready for Christmas – rehearsing carols and buying presents and decorations, and ordering festive food. I suppose there's an uneasy meeting ground in the threat of being overlooked by Santa Claus – who knows if you've been naughty or nice and won't stop by with your Christmas stocking if your conduct through the year didn't pass muster.

'Honestly, there's no wonder people don't believe in God any more, is there?' As the hill levels out along The Green, I put my thoughts into words. 'They get confused between Father Christmas not having any presents for you because you were mean to your little sister, and God having no place in heaven for you because you turned back the refugee at the border. It's simmered down into one big amorphous stew of vaguely threatening morality. God has certain standards in his expectations of us – or wait – is that Father Christmas? The more I think about it, the more it feels like a power game to me: controlling people's behaviour through punishment and reward.'

When Jesus doesn't reply at once, I throw a questioning glance in his direction. He nods, to let me know he's paying attention.

'I know what you mean,' he says, 'but it – all of it – was never meant as a threat. It was supposed to be a promise. The excitement of Father Christmas is surely about the joy of anticipating surprises – waking up to toys and sweets and new clothes on Christmas morning. These days before the winter solstice are about waiting . . . waiting . . . waiting for the Turn – Yul – when the infant light is born anew and life can breathe freely again.'

He stops speaking, but I can tell by his face it's just a pause. So I wait, expectantly, for what he wants to say, which is, finally: 'And judgement – well, that's not meant to be frightening. It's supposed to be something to look forward to: understanding at last, as truth shines out clear; healing at last, after struggling along with bad memories and old hurts and rotten systems. The judgement of God is always in our favour. God is never against us. The only time it's ever bad news is when someone's been relying on secrecy to run a scam or perpetuate abuse. If you're just honest and simple and doing your best, the judgement of God is a hand stretched out to help you, to lift you up, not smack you down. It's . . . judgement is an integral part of the Father's love.'

He sounds a bit upset, to me. I wonder if I should change the subject, or at least try to move things on.

'Perhaps,' I say, 'Mary riding slowly towards Bethlehem on the donkey, heavily pregnant, is the right picture of it.

Not so much a tyranny of expectations and 'Have we made the grade?' More the momentous excitement of expectancy, the imminent birth of a child. Advent resolves into the delivery into our hands of the greatest, dearest, sweetest gift of all – a child who simply needs our love, who wants to be fed and cuddled and welcomed, whose love is unconditional and expects nothing, but hopes for everything. Most of all, a child just wants to be with us. Does that sound right to you?'

'It sounds better than hell and damnation,' says Jesus. 'Because God sent his son into the world not to condemn the world, but so that through him the world might be saved.'

We've walked all the way through Silverhill and down Beaufort Road by this time, and I stand on the front step of our house with my hand on the doorknob.

'You are coming in?' I say to Jesus. 'You've still got time to stop by for a cup of tea?'

He smiles. 'Please,' he says. In fact, when I stop to think about it, every single time I've invited Jesus in, he has always said 'Yes'.

3

What it means to be with us

The Word became flesh and made his dwelling[1] among us.
We have seen his glory, the glory of the one and only Son,
who came from the Father, full of grace and truth.
(John 1.14 NIVUK)

This – the soft, dim interval as night gives on to day – this
is the quiet time. Before the world is stirring, when only the
voice of the crow cuts into awareness, before the dogs bark
and the children call out, here is the stillness in which light
is born.

We sit either side of the scrubbed table in the cold kitchen,
each with a mug of tea, the steam rising vague and sinuous
into the half light. Our kitchen window faces east, and outside the lilac and silver, the spreading flush of rose, harbingers the sun. In just a little while luminosity will streak
vivid aslant the horizon, but we are not there yet. We are
still waiting for the day. In the intimacy of this wintry hush,
Jesus is with me. I try not to snatch avidly at the opportunity; as always, I have so many questions, but I don't want
to splinter the peace that holds this space between night
and day.

Even so: 'Jesus,' I ask him, 'what does it even mean to call
you Emmanuel? People die in torture rooms. People commit

suicide. People starve. Sometimes they die in the rubble of buildings where the bombs have fallen. Sometimes they take forever to die, lying weeks, months, years on their own in the attic rooms of nursing homes, with a nurse coming in during the night and at intervals in the day to turn them, medicate them, push mush into their mouths with a spoon. All we know is that life is uncertain, and calamities can befall us and we can at a stroke lose everything. How . . . how are you with us?'

He does not speak. I glance at him across the table. He sits, quietly breathing, his face still.

'The thing is,' I say, 'I carry in my heart the awareness of so much suffering and injustice that I have no power to put right. I can pray, and sometimes I do but often I don't. And I find life difficult, Jesus. You walk on one side of me and the black dog walks on the other, and in my heart is the secret of longing for life to be over, and the dread of finding myself shut out of heaven.'

This is what I want to know: 'When I cannot see you, cannot feel you, are you still there? Will you always be with me? Or in the black flood of ending, will you let go of my hand?'

He picks up his mug, sips the steaming tea. The light of morning starts to dissolve the shadows of the room where we sit.

'I will not,' he says.

'Then . . . tell me how it works,' I beg him.

'Universe,' he says, 'is a word meaning "one turning". Everything folded and plaited and spiralled into a single being. We – it – everything – all now here. Everything that is proceeds from and belongs to God. There is no separation despite our myriad categorizations. The divisions are insignificant. Competition and warfare are senseless. Everything in the universe belongs to everything else, including you, so you can find all of it inside yourself. If you look outward, you perceive the teeming multitude of the ten thousand things, the branching, fractalling busyness of swarming life. From that point of view, I am to you a baby in a manger, or a man walking in the hills of Galilee, or a slumped body nailed to a cross. I become a thing, a moment, an instance, one note in a symphony. Maybe you can identify with me, maybe not, but I remain external to you when you look for me among the physical manifestations of life.

'The road home into the wellspring travels inward through your heart. If you can find the path inward, and focus on the origin and home of life, the heart of God, you cannot help but find me because I am there – and so are you. There is a way to allow the loneliness and grief, the physical disintegration of old age, the pain of loss and longing and even injustice, to keep their place in the rising and falling of external manifestations, while the core of you holds fast and steady to the road home, looking toward the source, keeping your feet in the way. It is, of course, not easy; but if you can master that discipline, you will always find me, because that's where I am.'

I try to absorb this. He takes another sip of his tea.

'There is no real sense in which you can lose me,' he adds, 'because I am here, and so are you. God is eternal life, and so is all that proceeds from God, because every single one of us can only make what we are – there are no other materials.

11

God is spirit, God is life, God is love; and God made you. God's spirit informs your self.'

Does this make sense? I'm not sure. But in some deep place inside, it comforts me. The buses roll out from the depot along the road from our house with a distant bass rumble, like Himalayan monks in their cavernous monastery chanting in the rising day. The sun is over the horizon. It's time to get on with life.

4

Judgement

I truly understand that God shows no partiality,
but in every nation anyone who fears him and does what is right
is acceptable to him. You know the message he sent to the people
of Israel, preaching peace by Jesus Christ—he is Lord of all. . . .
He commanded us to preach to the people and to testify that
he is the one ordained by God as judge of the living and the dead.
All the prophets testify about him that everyone who believes
in him receives forgiveness of sins through his name.
(Acts 10.34-36, 42-43 NRSV)

The bitter cold of the year usually arrives in January. After the storms of October and November have subsided panting, their work of shaking and ripping every leaf from the trees complete, there often comes this calm and mild spell in December, when it's nice to go out for a walk. And so it is today. We go Indian file down the steps and narrow path strewn with dark, sodden leaves, descending into the valley with the duck pond at the bottom, where we take a while to sit on the park bench watching squirrels chasing each other along the branches of a Scots pine, and enjoy the sunlight dancing on the rippled surface of the pond.

There is an immense quietness that emanates from Jesus. Once you have sat next to him, you will never need anyone to explain to you what peace can be. It is as though all of life comes to rest in his presence, the whole chaotic tangle settles down.

I do not know how this can be. Nothing changes. The same political wrangling and media posturing and rampant consumerism tearing the guts out of the earth remain in place. There's no more money in the current account or food in the fridge than before. The pervasive shades of mediocrity and failure continue to reign supreme in my life – which is like a painting done entirely in sage green and mauve, managing to be even more obscure and insignificant than a space on the wall. Grey is eye-catching by comparison. And yet, when I sit beside Jesus, the familiar existential ache stops hurting. The realities that frame my world cease to hem me in. Here, with him, I am content to simply be; everything's all right.

And what puzzles me about this is the concept of Christ being my judge. I look at the calm composure of his face, his gaze blessing the water, the birds, the trees, the clouds, the day, and I try to imagine him saying, 'Depart from me; I never knew you,' or banishing me to eternal hellfire because I didn't put enough of what I could afford into the food bank and I stopped visiting my Granny. You know, there are some really troubling things written in the Bible.

'D'you want to talk about it?' he asks. Evidently the stirring of my restless questions is as palpable to him as his peace is to me.

'Well . . .' This feels slightly awkward to broach. 'My mind was boggling at the prospect that you might . . . that you could . . . send me to Hell.'

I don't typically think through in advance what another person's reaction might be. I just say what happens to be passing through my head and see how we go. Even so, I register a certain inner surprise when he doesn't even move, doesn't turn his head – just goes right on letting his gaze rest on the water.

After a moment, 'I'm not going to send you anywhere,' he says.

'No?' I have to challenge this. 'Dives and Lazarus? Sheep and goats? Christ our judge?'

He takes a deep breath and lets it go in a sigh, not impatient, more . . . tired, I think. Does Jesus get tired? I don't know.

'The thing is,' he says, 'it's not about me lording it over you. Judgement arises inside you. If you say something unkind, you know it's unkind; it doesn't need someone to tell you. You are human; you know how it is to feel lonely and hungry and cold, to be worried and ill, and what a difference it makes if someone stops to help you. You exercise your own judgement. You allocate your resources accordingly. You build your own future. You help create either one kind of world or a different one. If you stop and think about it, you know who you are and what you're building, and whether it will be hell or heaven. But it's made by you, by the daily, hour-by-hour exercise of your own judgement. It's not about sending anyone to hell. It can't work like that, if you think about it. There are some people who would turn anywhere into hell for everybody else if they're given the chance, while there are others it would be impossible to send to hell, because it would no longer be hell once they got there: they'd turn it around.'

I watch a pair of ducks fly in and land on the water. 'So it's up to me? Judgement is the voice of truth inside me? What about when I'm harassed and have too much to think about and make poor choices, then?'

He nods. 'Yes. That's all part of the responsibility of being a disciple though, isn't it? Give yourself the space you need to make wise decisions. But I do understand. You are only human. Sometimes you get it wrong. Bear in mind, that as well as judgement, there is also mercy, and it has no time limit on it. God's mercy never runs out.'

The quietness expands and laps around me. I can't figure out if he's just made this easier or twice as hard.

5

Dominion

A dispute also arose among them, which of them was to be regarded as the greatest. And he said to them, 'The kings of the Gentiles exercise lordship over them; and those in authority over them are called benefactors. But not so with you; rather let the greatest among you become as the youngest, and the leader as one who serves. For which is the greater, one who sits at table, or one who serves? Is it not the one who sits at table? But I am among you as one who serves.
(Luke 22.24-27 RSV)

In the kitchen, waiting for the kettle to boil, I stare out of the window, lost in thought. In my opinion, one of the many unhelpful things the church ever did was coin its first creed, 'Jesus is Lord.' I mean, how confrontational and divisive and antagonistic is that? In the great playground of faith, along comes a new child and gives the others a shove. What happens? Another religious war breaks out, people fed to the lions and burned at the stake. Humanity is an aggressive and competitive race. Everyone wants to be king of the castle.

So my attention is recalled by the kettle now boiling madly, and I go back to what I was doing – making a cup of tea for Jesus. I know by this time exactly how he likes his tea, which makes me happy. Strong, if you want to know, and milky. Tea gives me indigestion, so I drink a nettle brew. I take our steaming mugs through to the living room, where I find him kneeling by the hearth laying the fire.

'You must have been a big help to your mother,' I say as I put our mugs down on the table.

Jesus is good at lighting fires – and at finding lost things. He must have been useful at home. I have discovered he also has talent at bending time and changing minds, areas where most people struggle.

He gets the fire going nicely and reaches for his mug of tea. 'Thank you,' he says. I curl up on the sofa, and Jesus sits on the floor by the fire.

'Dominion,' I remark, by way of getting a conversation started, 'is a big problem. That first shot at a creed, *Jesus is Lord*, was distinctly unhelpful. Wasn't it?'

'The way you just said it, yes,' he replies. 'But they didn't mean it like that. They intended not "Jesus is *Lord*", but "*Jesus* is Lord"'.

'What?' I stare at him, baffled. 'How is that an improvement?'

'It's meant to be about what I stood for,' he says. 'You have to think of "Jesus" as a summarizing of "love, patience, humility, laying down your life".'

He sips his tea, and he asks me, 'Have you read the Gospels?'

'Of course I have! What's that supposed to mean?' Is Jesus picking an argument with me?

'Then you'll have noticed,' he says quietly, ignoring my indignation, 'the extreme difficulty I had in trying to reconfigure people's understanding about the nature of Messiah. That it wasn't about being cock of the walk, more about being the sea to which all streams flow easily because it lies below them. I wanted them to see that leadership is not about ordering people about, but taking responsibility. Authority arises from being the one who will go and do what has to be done – and grit your teeth to bear the pain that's part of the package. It's more like the mother who, when times are hard, without a word passes her last crust to her hungry child, than like the king who – also when times are hard – sucks the livelihood out of his people in taxes.

'They didn't get it,' he says. 'Right to the last they didn't get it. Arguing and jostling for position, grabbing palm branches and shouting hosanna to make a political figurehead out of me. They wanted a little king, a partisan hero, a man who would take up their cause against all the others – and emerge triumphant, holding his trophy in the air and dispatching his enemies. What I wanted was so much bigger, so much more than that, they couldn't even conceptualize it. I wanted something that would work for all humanity. Something that would be healing – salvation – for *everyone*. And to get to that. you have to go down low. You have to be the deep lake in the valley, not the jaunty little spring at the top of the hill. Love goes down low, humility does. That's what "*Jesus* is Lord" means, that lowliness is central to dominion. If you take out of any situation the willingness to bear responsibility, to help and heal and love and serve, then you haven't got "Jesus is Lord" any more. You've taken the Jesus out of it. What you have left is whatever else you put into it instead – "Posturing is Lord" or "Image is Lord" or "Mammon is Lord" or "The Church is Lord". You can't use my name if you don't walk my path. It simply cannot work like that. If you're asking me, I think it's fine as a creed, but the first people who have to live by it are the people who proclaim it. It doesn't mean anything at all if it's used to tyrannize other people and rubbish other paths of faith.'

'Oh.' I think about this for a minute. You know, there is something profoundly calming about watching Jesus drinking tea and gazing thoughtfully into the fire. 'So . . . what about the exclusive claims of the gospel? Things you actually said yourself. Like, "I am the way, the truth and the life. No one comes to the Father but by me"?'

He glances at me. 'It's true,' he says. 'It's absolutely true. The new and living way I made is *myself*. The labels people put on it are not so very important, but you can take it from me, there is no way to heaven except my way – humility, the willingness to serve and to take responsibility, allowing yourself to be vulnerable, giving yourself to love. There's no other way. If you're doing that, then you *are* with me.'

6

Vulnerability

Three different times I begged God to make me well again.
Each time he said, 'No. But I am with you; that is all you need.
My power shows up best in weak people.' Now I am glad to boast
about how weak I am; I am glad to be a living demonstration
of Christ's power, instead of showing off my own power and abilities.
Since I know it is all for Christ's good, I am quite happy
about 'the thorn,' and about insults and hardships, persecutions
and difficulties; for when I am weak, then I am strong—
the less I have, the more I depend on him.
(2 Corinthians 12.8-10 *The Living Bible*)

Sometimes I can drive a car and sometimes it's too much for me, because what I call my Mental Elf lives in a state of constant fluctuation. Just now I'm sitting on the bus as it chugs up the long hill from the sea and stops by the old hospital to let a straggle of people on board. There, patiently queuing behind the bent old lady with a shopping trolley and the young mum with a toddler in a pushchair, stands Jesus.

I feel a sudden surge of alarm. The thing is, Jesus never has any money with him. How am I going to get to him and pay his fare if the bus aisle is blocked by one woman struggling to dock a trolley and another manoeuvring a stroller?

But since it's Jesus, obviously I have to try. So I leap to my feet and battle my way to the driver's cab, apologizing and tripping over things on the way. Arriving panting at the driver's elbow, I say, 'I'll pay this man's fare.'

The driver turns his head to give me a long, puzzled look. He says, 'What man?'

Not everyone is aware of the presence of Jesus. I know dogs and small children can reliably see him, but plenty of adults simply don't know he's there. And this is my worst nightmare now, as I watch the bus driver's expression change to something softer, something gentle and kind. He says to me, 'It's okay, love. He doesn't need a ticket.'

Furious, embarrassed, red-faced, muttering thank-yous and apologies, I muddle back to my seat, Jesus following close behind. I'm not going to talk to him now. What if nobody else can see him either? Every single person on the bus will think I'm mad, not just the bus driver. And I hate it. I do have a Mental Elf problem, but I go to immense lengths to keep it private and appear as sane as I possibly can. For a moment I'm so wrapped up in the humiliation of it all that I'm hardly aware of Jesus myself, until he gives me a little nudge and says, 'Thank you for offering.'

So the bus rattles on through the lights and we get off at the supermarket and stand by the crossing, waiting patiently for the green man because this junction is massive and it's not safe to chance it; you just have to wait for the pedestrian light to go green. Surrounded by a dense clump of the usual Silverhill raggle-taggle of sharp-eyed shabby people – one woman herding a man who's rocking and clutching a blue plastic ball to help him concentrate and stand still – I'm still not speaking to Jesus. I'm not in a sulk; I just don't want anybody else to think I'm out of my mind. I've spent my entire life trying to keep vulnerability hidden and I'm not about to muck it up for anyone, not even Jesus. I notice the rocking man with the ball has half-turned and is darting furtive glances at Jesus, who smiles at him, and the man's face lights up in a sudden grin of delight. And then the crossing beeper starts and we all surge forward. Jesus and I cross again by the hospice shop and pass the kebab shop and the pub all shrouded in scaffolding and plastic sheets for builders to address their leaky roofs. Then we gain the peace of our quiet road, all strewn with blown leaves from the park – once the street sweepers would have cleared these in the fall, but times are hard and the council is on a tight budget.

Now, as we walk along side by side, Jesus says to me, 'You know, I will always be with you. I know what it's like to be alone and scared, to be disregarded. I've been there. My family tried to section me, and most of the people who didn't laugh at me thought I was a danger to society.'

I suppose that's true.

Then he says, 'Cultivating an image, a protective shell, is not really the most effective way to manage vulnerability. It does take courage to walk a precarious path, even when that's not a personal choice but all life offers you. The best way is to cultivate trust. If you cannot trust yourself, well, you can still trust me. And I do mean it – I am always with you. I won't let you down.'

I guess that's what he was getting at when he said, not Jesus is *Lord* but *Jesus* is Lord. It isn't about conquering and bullying through, much less about trying to keep up appearances. It's about being able to make peace with who you are, because you know Jesus is there even if no one else does – and you know you can trust him even when all else fails. It's not that he lifts you out of the place where you are; he just comes to find you there and travels with you, as vulnerable as you are yourself yet somehow transforming everything, because that's what you do if you are Lord.

7

The prophetic life

This is what was spoken through the prophet Joel:
  'In the last days it will be, God declares,
   that I will pour out my Spirit upon all flesh,
and your sons and your daughters shall prophesy,
    and your young men shall see visions,
    and your old men shall dream dreams.
 Even upon my slaves, both men and women,
    in those days I will pour out my Spirit;
        and they shall prophesy.'
        (Acts 2.16-18 NRSVA)

We were going to watch 'Homes under the Hammer', but a thought has been nagging at me, and I sit there with the remote control held idly in my hand. 'Jesus,' I say, 'I have a question.'

I'm not entirely sure Jesus shares my enthusiasm for 'Homes under the Hammer'. His eyes brighten now. 'Go on,' he says, with a sudden kindling of interest.

'It's about the prophetic life,' I tell him. 'Because the thing is, I'm not sure I've got one. I mean, we're all meant to show forth the gospel and offer an active witness to our generation, aren't we? We're supposed to give an account of the faith within us and share the good news with our fellow human beings. But in my case, there's a definite snag. Nobody's interested in what I have to say. I am a complete nonentity. If I started giving an account of the faith inside me, it would only irritate people. On the whole I think they'd rather it stayed inside me and I left them in peace. And I can't do prophetic actions by helping refugees and the poor or setting up women's refuges and educating orphans in war-torn countries, because I haven't got any money. I suppose buying locally grown organic food is a little bit prophetic, because it works towards the peaceable kingdom and extends the shalom of God, but that and going to church are frankly the best I can manage – and I can't always face the going to church. Am I let off the hook for living a prophetic life, or is there something I'm missing?'

Jesus laughs. 'Let off the hook? You wish! Yes, sometimes I had a longing for that option. Short answer is, no, you are not. So long as you have breath in your body, your mission on earth is not complete.'

'So . . . ?' I look at him hopefully. Maybe I have a contribution to make after all, in accomplishing the transformative purposes of God.

'You've got it the wrong way round,' he says. 'You're looking at the bowl not the soup, if you see what I mean. Looking at the fuel not the flame. You're focusing on the circumstances instead of the active spirit.'

I have nothing to say about this. He looks at me to check if I'm keeping up, and I just nod helpfully. I think my incomprehension doesn't escape him.

'If you think about yesterday,' he says, 'what happened during the day?'

I consider this. 'Absolutely zilch,' I say, but he's shaking his head.

'In the morning,' he reminds me, 'you prayed for your mother, struggling with the uphill climb to the end of her earthly life. You can't see the difference that made, but I assure you it did. You held her in the light, and that's a prophetic act. It says prayer makes a difference, and so it does. Always. You also resolved to withdraw from the matrix of tricky dynamics at church, so as not to escalate delicate relationships into antagonisms. That's also a prophetic act; it promotes peace and humility, respect for your sisters and brothers in the gospel. When the deliveryman came with a parcel, you opened the door to him with a smile and asked how his day was going, and remembered his name and thanked him. That's a prophetic act. It told him he is worth something as an individual – you spoke for God to him. And you fed the crow an entire sausage. Remember? We stood in the garden watching him fly back to his family with it gripped firmly in his claws. That's a prophetic act. It announces that we all belong to one another in the family of creation; we are here to watch out for each other. The prophetic life doesn't mean standing on a podium at Hyde Park Corner declaiming to the crowd and fielding the comments of hecklers. Not everyone is John the Baptist; in fact, now I come to think of it, one of him was probably plenty. A little of my cousin John went a very long way. The prophetic life doesn't need a platform; it only needs the practice of kindness and a discipline of love. It doesn't even have to be seen or heard; it only needs to be lived.'

He stops, checks in with me again, and yes, I'm still listening.

'There's something else,' he says. 'Not many aspects of the life of faith belong to isolation. It's a family thing, a community thing; the household of faith makes its pilgrimage all together. The communion of saints and all that. It's like an orchestra. Not everyone is the conductor or the first violin. In any given piece, the French horn player maybe gets to go "parp" every few bars and that's their lot. You can hardly hear the harp with the kettledrums rolling. Or it's like a choir – the sopranos generally get to hold the melody and you couldn't ignore the tenors if you wanted to. Maybe you're an alto filling in the harmony, or the bass underpinning the thing. But nobody who knows anything about symphonies or choral music would make the mistake of sending the altos and the second bassoon back home. Are they part of it? Do they make a difference? You bet!

'Nobody has to do the whole thing, and everybody's contribution is part of the music. The church is not all about the preacher and the organist. The person who prepared the notices sheet and the person who handed it to you with a smile as you came in, they are just as important. When the spirit was poured out on all flesh at Pentecost, we moved on from the days of the solo prophet. The prophetic life is seen in the whole people of God. And even if all you do is play the triangle in this grand orchestration, that does mean you as well. You're hired. You belong. What you put in matters. Every angel in heaven notices if you take the day off.'

As I take this in, my gaze drifts across the room to the clock on the piano. This is good news, isn't it; but is it worth tuning in to 'Homes under the Hammer' for the last eight minutes? Probably not.

8

Candles

You're here to be light, bringing out the God-colors in the world.
God is not a secret to be kept. We're going public with this,
as public as a city on a hill. If I make you light-bearers,
you don't think I'm going to hide you under a bucket, do you?
I'm putting you on a light stand. Now that I've put you there
on a hilltop, on a light stand—shine! Keep open house; be generous
with your lives. By opening up to others, you'll prompt people
to open up with God, this generous Father in heaven.
(Matthew 5.14-16 The Message)

Jesus is very practical. Somehow I managed to live several decades of my life without even noticing this. 'Practical' is not a word I associate with Jesus. 'Visionary', yes, or 'inspirational'. When I think about it, I realize I've acquired and assembled a concept of Jesus as essentially airy-fairy—a stern and preoccupied gaze resting on the middle distance while an inscrutable smile plays tantalizingly about his lips. Five minutes in the company of Jesus as he actually is blows these fatuous notions clean out of the water. Jesus is down to earth. He is realistic. His spirituality plugs in to the here and now, securely connecting heaven to this world, this place, these circumstances.

We stand in the very small aisle running alongside the massive display of Christmas paraphernalia in the discount warehouse. It has every permutation of cheap bauble made in Hong Kong you can possibly imagine, enough tinsel to throw twice round the moon, an assortment of wall-eyed reindeers leaning drunkenly upon each other for support, and on the shelf in front of us a variety of LED candles – tall pillar candles made of real wax with a flickering bulb halfway down the inside, and the imitation plastic tea lights with fitfully flickering flame-shaped bulbs on the top. I'm considering getting a box of these for the crib service.

I ask him doubtfully, 'What d'you think? Should we have these, or is it better to have real candles?'

Even as I frame the question, I think I know what his answer will be. Jesus is all about authenticity, isn't he? How likely is it, after all, that Jesus is going to pick an imitation plastic anything over the real thing?

Beeswax candles clean the air as they burn, unlike paraffin wax. They release negative ions, neutralizing the positive ions in fumes and dirt so they just drop to the ground – unlike paraffin candles, which give off more chemicals than you can shake a stick at. Beeswax smells heavenly. Paraffin candles do not. I would put money on Jesus going for nothing but ethically produced, one hundred per cent pure beeswax every time without fail. But he always surprises me.

Jesus is the veteran of innumerable acts of worship. As we weigh up the possibilities, he reminds me of the time we actually managed to set the sanctuary carpet on fire during the Taizé service at St George's Church at Brede, and I had to crawl about as unobtrusively as I could, whacking the tea lights with the Birkenstock sandal I'd snatched off my foot to stop the whole thing going up in a conflagration. The carpet was nylon, and the little metal holders got too hot as the wax burned down.

He says, 'These candles are to give out to little children, right?' We run various scenarios, considering the work the steward has to do after the service finishes, crawling about on his hands and knees scraping the drips of wax off the carpet. We take a moment of silence to imagine even one little girl with long hair leaning over the lit flame to say something to her mother. Hair makes mighty fine kindling.

When Jesus was a child, everyone had oil lamps or beeswax candles; everyone cooked over the fire. Naked flames belonged to the everyday world; you drummed vigilance into every little kid as a first principle – 'Look what you're doing, mind that lamp, hold that steady, not too near'.

As we mull over our options now, he points out that though mass-produced plastic tea lights are hardly earth-friendly, we have to work with the people we've got, and it's always better not to set anybody on fire. Then, 'Oh, look,' he says. 'Have you seen these ones?' He's found a pack of tea lights with a plug-in charging base, so you don't have to keep getting new batteries.

'Jesus,' I say, 'you're a genius! That's absolutely perfect.'

As we queue at the checkout, idly watching the automated penguins singing pop songs in the window display, Jesus says, 'You were right about real candles – I do like them best, because they come from the life of bees; they have summer in them and they smell of honey. They are beautiful because they arise from the earth. A living flame is a sort of prayer all by itself. It's warm and vital. Everything that's alive has danger in it, is unpredictable. It can hurt you, or be extinguished and quenched; it can burn a hole in the order of service; it can drip wax onto your trousers. Anything that's real and alive requires you to pay attention. But . . .'

It's our turn to pay, and because this is a discount store full of cheap trash from China, the total comes in low enough for a contactless payment, which is a relief. 'But what?' I ask him as we thank the cashier and make our way out into the night.

'Well, you have to be responsible and considerate about it, don't you? The crib service is for the youngest children. People should have a nice time in church. It should leave them with a happy memory. Church shouldn't hurt people, shouldn't leave them with their fingers burned. Church shouldn't leave you with scars. It's meant to include you, to be accessible and welcoming. Church is meant to be for everybody, no one left out. If that means fake candles, well, so be it. Loving is always about compromise, isn't it? You have to start with the people, surely, not with the traditions and the liturgy.'

'Ha!' We thread our way to the back of the queue lining up by the bus shelter. 'I wish everyone thought like you do!'

9

Singing

The Son is the image of the invisible God, the firstborn
over all creation. For in him all things were created:
things in heaven and on earth, visible and invisible,
whether thrones or powers or rulers or authorities;
all things have been created through him and for him.
He is before all things, and in him all things hold together . . .
For God was pleased to have all his fullness dwell in him,
and through him to reconcile to himself all things,
whether things on earth or things in heaven,
by making peace through his blood, shed on the cross.
(Colossians 1.15-17,19-20 NIV UK)

On what were [the earth's] *footings set,*
or who laid its cornerstone –
while the morning stars sang together
and all the angels shouted for joy?
(Job 38.6-7 NIV UK)

I don't know why, but I always assumed Jesus would sing
the tune – the melody line. It came as a shock of pleasure to stand next to him singing in church and discover
he puts in the harmonies. I guess your average man isn't
confident enough to hold the tenor line or the bass, but

Jesus – well, he's heard a lot of hymns in the past two millennia, has he not? He seems to know them all, anyway.

I ask him, 'Will you come carol-singing at the supermarket with us this year?' And he says he will; he loves to join in and he's looking forward to it. So now something's puzzling me.

'Jesus,' I say, 'you know how not everyone can see you, or presumably hear you either? What will that mean about the carol-singing? Will only some of the people be able to hear you sing? The children and a handful of others?'

'Probably,' he says. 'That's generally the way of it.'

I find this really disappointing. 'That's such a pity. I love your voice. I want everyone to hear you. And besides, we need all the help we can get, there's only the six of us.'

He smiles. 'You know how it is,' he says. 'If I sing with you, it makes a difference even if bystanders don't know I'm there. You have your own voice – you are your own unique self, but at the same time I sing through you, if you know what I mean. I'm *with* you, and that strengthens what belongs to you.'

Oh, yes. I know exactly what he means. His companionship is entirely transformative. It's like I'm a different person, somehow, when I'm alongside Jesus.

'Even so,' I persist, 'it'll be a pity for people who hear us to miss the harmonies you're singing.'

There is this kind of quizzical expression in his eyes sometimes. 'What?' I say. 'What? Am I failing to notice something?'

'I think you might be,' he says. 'All creation is always singing. Birds, obviously, but the stars sing too. There's the song of the sea and the song of the dawn. The vibration of everything that is harmonizes in the most glorious choral song and finds its keynote and its resonance in me. I hold all creation together in a harmonic balance of reconciliation in my heart. Nothing can sing without me, and where they lift their voice in song, I am the music. The melody of life runs through my heart.'

I frown. 'Some people sing badly out of tune,' I point out. 'What happens to their harmonic resonance? Do they let go of it?'

Jesus laughs. 'No,' he says, 'they don't. It's something deeper than musical ability; it's a location of the soul. Where our roots go. The song of creation is like an interconnective mycelium, a web of joy and power running through the whole of life and joining it all up.'

This rings a bell somewhere far back in my memory. 'Wait . . . isn't that . . .' I concentrate hard, trying to remember. 'Isn't this something to do with quantum physics? Everything that lives having its own vibrational frequency, and all frequencies vibrating on a plane? And that . . . the harmony of the vibration is what makes everything seem solid and real – because we're actually made up of energy, light, sound, but we all hold together? I'm sorry, Jesus, I am no physicist, as my high school teachers made clear to me in no uncertain terms. But this is the part of the wood where physics morphs into theology, isn't it?'

'It helps,' says Jesus, 'to be comfortable with mystery.'

'It's coming back to me now! That the physical is only one plane of vibration, and the source energy vibrates at such a high level you might as well say it's at rest. And understanding and managing the energy is the basis of spiritual discipline. Is that – have I got it right?'

Jesus smiles. 'There are,' he says, 'no beginnings and endings. There is just the one song. What you may be more used to thinking of as the Word of God. From this, light proceeds, and love. It is grace in the world. It is both holy and entirely natural. But, what I wanted to say to you is that if you can hit this frequency when you go carol-singing, it won't matter who can see and hear me and who can't, because we will be singing in harmony. The people coming into the store won't analyse what's happening; they will only know that somehow it makes them feel happy.'

I like the sound of that. 'So . . . you'll be there?' I just want to be sure.

'Yes,' says Jesus. 'I will. I'll be singing with you.'

10

Fire

*People's hopes began to rise, and they began to wonder whether
John perhaps might be the Messiah. So John said to all of them,
'I baptise you with water, but someone is coming who is much
greater than I am. I am not good enough even to untie his sandals.
He will baptise you with the Holy Spirit and fire.*
(Luke 3.15-16 GNT)

*I came to set the earth on fire, and how I wish it were already
kindled! I have a baptism to receive, and how distressed I am until
it is over! Do you suppose that I came to bring peace to the world?
No, not peace, but division.*
(Luke 49—51 GNT)

I think of our fire as a domestic dragon. It is alive, it needs
to breathe, it has to be fed. Like all living creatures, it is
to some degree dangerous and unpredictable. If it got out
of the confines of its basket, there would be monumental
destruction in our living room within seconds. But I love
our fire, in the way you can only love a living being.

I left Jesus sitting by the fire while I went to the kitchen to
make him a cup of tea. Bringing two steaming mugs to the
fireside with me, I push the door more nearly closed with
my foot, to keep the warmth in.

'Be careful,' I say, as I hand him his mug of tea. 'It's hot.'

In silence, ideas grow. All kinds of thoughts flourish and develop in silence. As we sit together without speaking, watching the dancing flames and falls of ash, I think about fire in the Bible. Most of it sounds terrifying. Ananias, Azarias and Misael thrown into the burning, fiery furnace. The elements melting in the heat. Dives begging Abraham to send Lazarus to dip his finger in some water to cool off Dives' tongue, because he's in agony in the fire of Hades. People cast alive into a lake of fire in the book of Revelation. The word of God burning like a fire shut up in Jeremiah's bones. The angel coming with a live coal to touch Isaiah's lips. None of this is even faintly attractive. When I sit by the fireside on a winter's night – or cook sausages over a fire pit in the garden on a summer day – it's such a happy thing. I associate it with contentment, the way life should be. I love the smell of a fire; our entire house has a clinging fragrance of woodsmoke. But fire in the Bible is ominous and agonizing. Even Jesus cooking fish at the lakeside after the resurrection is unsettling – it's not as if they were *expecting* him to be there. And at Pentecost the Spirit comes as a rushing mighty wind and tongues of flame. If that combination isn't the start of trouble, I don't know what is. This is not discipleship for the Highly Sensitive Person, is it?

'It's an art.' Jesus speaks quietly into my uneasy, unspoken thoughts. 'It requires vigilance and understanding. If you walk in the way of the Spirit, you become a living torch. The fire is inside you. Fire is not afraid of itself. When you walk through the fire, I will be with you. You will not be burned; you will be yourself a flame. The fire of the Spirit cleanses and purifies; it warms and heals. But it is true that it hurts terribly sometimes, and there's nothing you can do then but humbly endure it.'

'What does it mean,' I ask him, 'that you will baptize us with Holy Spirit and fire? How does that happen?'

He blows his tea thoughtfully, takes an experimental sip and thinks better of it, sets the mug down on the hearthstone. 'Baptism,' he says, 'is immersion. You go right in. You stand up to your waist in living water, and then somebody takes you right down in over your head. My baptism – the Holy Spirit and fire one – is about finding the courage to enter the living stream of Spirit, the river of fire and light, the flow of love. You can't just *paddle* in discipleship – it doesn't work like that. The way of faith isn't a hobby. You don't need to be afraid of it, but yes, it is complete immolation. It is a holocaust of sorts.'

'Jesus,' I protest, 'that sounds absolutely awful. To be honest, I'm surprised you have any followers at all.'

I look at his hands linked loosely together, restful, at peace. My experience of him has been so gentle and healing. I'm frightened now. Are there awful things ahead? Is my life going to be ruined? Is the choice between the inferno of the Spirit and the burning torture of hell?

'The art of it,' he says, 'lies in becoming the flame. You are burning, but you are not being burned. The fuel is not you, but all the dross and rubbish your life has accumulated, dead grass and fallen branches. What is burning up is everything that is not alive, the food for the fire. As you identify yourself with me and we become one, all the nonsense and prevarication and pretence has to be refined out of existence. You cannot serve God and Mammon; you have to let go, be entirely surrendered. How could that be easy? But even so, it is natural. It's what you were born to be: a beacon, a lantern, a light for the world. A candle isn't itself until it's kindled. Until someone puts a match to it, there's nothing but a stick of wax in a box.'

I feel unsettled and worried now. How am I going to do this, live up to this? I don't think I want to be set on fire.

'I am with you,' he says. 'That's all it is. Everyone who travels with me sooner or later catches fire. They can't help it. The Spirit is alive and alight. I think the bottom line is you have to trust me. You have to love me. You have to want to be with me.'

And of course I do.

11

Frost

[Jesus said] 'The sheep hear his voice, and he calls his own sheep
by name and leads them out. When he has brought out all his own,
he goes before them, and the sheep follow him, for they know
his voice. A stranger they will not follow, but they will flee from him,
for they do not know the voice of strangers.'. . .
So Jesus again said to them, 'Truly, truly, I say to you,
I am the door of the sheep . . . I am the door; if any one enters by me,
he will be saved, and will go in and out and find pasture . . .
I came that they may have life, and have it abundantly . . .
I am the good shepherd. I know my own, and my own know me.'
(John 10 RSV, a selection of verses from the passage running 1-18;
I encourage you to look it up and read the whole thing.)

I didn't always live here, in this town by the sea. In my childhood our family moved from place to place, but my favourite
of our homes was a thirteenth-century house on the out-
skirts of a country village. It was while we lived there that I
first got to know Jesus. I'd heard about him, of course, but I
met him for myself then. We had a huge garden – five acres
– with a river running through it. The ground rose steeply in
a protective encircling belt of woodland around the paddock
where gypsies kept their parti-coloured horses and where
later we grazed sheep.

Last thing at night and first thing in the morning we'd go out to shut in the hens and check on the sheep, see that all was well. I remember especially the frosty nights, the sheep snuggled close together in their byre at the foot of the curving hillside of bare winter trees, the wild rabbits in the moonlight nibbling the frozen grass, everything so quiet and clear and cold. It was beautiful.

That was long ago and far away, but here on the hilltop by the sea, I still like to go outside on a winter's night and look up at the shining moon and feel the invigoration of the frosty air. Tonight I stand with Jesus under the stars.

I say to him, 'This – the cold and the firmament of stars, and the rising moon, the snap of frost in the air and the quietness of night – this feeds my soul. I come out here and shut the door behind me, and I feel the beauty and the freshness nourishing my spirit.'

He doesn't reply, and his silence speaks but I can't read it. 'What?' I ask him.

'Well,' he says carefully, 'I don't want to put a damper on anything – it *is* beautiful. But part of what makes it so special and magical is the contrast. Leaving the warm house with the evening lamps and the fire burning, and coming outside to stand in the wildness of the frosty night – always knowing you can go in again when you've had enough and you're getting chilly. Going outside feeds your soul, but being able to go back in is comfortable and restful and makes you feel safe. I was only thinking I wish everyone had both.'

Yes. I think about refugees in hopelessly inadequate footwear and flimsy tents, harassed from place to place with nowhere to call home, fleeing violence and destruction, poverty and desertification. I imagine them with trench foot, camping in flip-flops on this night of frost and stars, with nothing to sustain them but a cellphone and their stubborn human hope; and I wish they could come indoors to somewhere they called home.

I think about the stealth campers dotted around our town in their vans, the windows curtained or blocked with aluminium sunshields to disguise the presence of someone living inside, huddled over a cup of tea as the cold closes in. One step up from a sleeping bag in a shop doorway.

The inside and the outside belong together, don't they? Exodus becomes exile when you have nowhere to call home. There isn't the same freedom in the great outdoors when the whole earth offers you no friendly fireside, and there is no welcome for you.

'Foxes have their holes and birds have their nests,' I quote his own words back to him, 'but the Son of Man had nowhere to lay his head.'

'"Has",' he corrects me. 'It is still my business to seek and to save the lost. It is still true that what you do to the least of these, you do to me. And before you start arguing with me, let me say I know the human race; I do understand that it is politically very difficult. I know well that your house is full, and your pocket is empty. But still my heart breaks for the wanderers who have nowhere to go home. And I am with them.'

I can find no words for this. It's cold, and I want to go in now, but this doesn't seem the moment to say so. To set the prisoner free and bring the lost home is the longing of the heart of Jesus. This I know. I end the long, moonlit silence

by asking him, 'What can I do? It's what you said yourself –
the poor will always be with us.'

He nods. 'They will. The poor and the lost. And the kingdom is built one home, one meal, one smile at a time. Give
what you can.'

Later, when we've gone inside and closed the door against
the night, sitting by the warmth of the fire in the hearth, he
adds, 'You know, there is also a way of being with people
that helps them come home whatever their circumstances
may be. You cannot always mend a broken situation, but
you can make them a home in your heart. By the choices
you make and the person you become, you can weave the
fabric of welcome and reconciliation. It's the love that makes
a building a home and not a prison. And it's love that sets
people free instead of driving them away. That's the thing to
work on. You can afford to love.'

12

Starlight

And God said, 'Let there be lights in the vault of the sky
to separate the day from the night, and let them serve as signs
to mark sacred times, and days and years.'
(Genesis 1.14 NIV UK)

I consider thy heavens, the work of thy fingers,
the moon and the stars, which thou hast ordained.
(Psalm 8.3-4 KJV)

Now when Jesus was born in Bethlehem of Judaea in the days
of Herod the king, behold, there came wise men from the east
to Jerusalem, saying, Where is he that is born King of the Jews?
for we have seen his star in the east, and are come to worship him.
(Matthew 2.1-2 KJV)

There's that brief time as day turns toward evening and
dusk falls when everything shines. In summer the colour
of the flowers intensifies and glows, and their fragrance
diffuses through the dying day. Now in the winter, though
shadows deepen into mystery under the yews and among
the pines, where stillness breathes in silence, as we walk
along the paths of the park in the last of the light, every
scarlet berry and every leaf still clinging golden and

crimson to the naked branches of the deciduous trees is shining.

Then as the wing of evening brushes low and the light begins to fail, I can see Venus glowing resplendent with her lustrous beauty above the horizon to the southwest, the evening star. I know Saturn is close by her, low above the brim of the world, but I'd really need binoculars to pick him out, and they're at home. At this time of year, Jupiter is lost in the twilight, and I'll only see the warm light of Mars if I happen to wake three hours before the dawn. Even then, he is far from the earth just now, and hard to see. There, to the east of Venus, the brightness of a full moon already rising. And all this while Jesus says not a word, but he is with me and we walk together. This day has the earliest sunset of the year. It is the first official day of winter. Nearer the solstice, I know that if I'm out at the right time and place, I may catch a glimpse of Earthshine on the moon's waning crescent.

'Jesus,' I ask him, as we begin to climb the steep hill toward home, 'what are the stars for?'

He answers me after a moment. 'How do you mean? The stars are not for anything. They are alive.'

'Well, are they . . . do they *mean* something? Do they tell us anything? Are they . . . is astrology just rubbish? What are the stars?'

Jesus considers my question. This is in any case not a good point on the hill to start a conversation. Trying to walk and talk has left me out of breath. Jesus is well used to walking, but even so he waits until we get to the level ground before he replies. 'You might do better,' he says, 'to think of a star as a person more than a thing. A star is more of a *Who* than a *What*, in truth. Just as you are a populated world as well as a self, and just as you have your place in humanity, and you are rooted in and arise from God, so it is with the stars. They turn in their courses within the great plan and pattern of life, and they are beings as well as worlds, just as you are.'

He's right, of course, as always. I think of myself as just me, but I am a whole world in a sense. Trillions of microscopic organisms live in me, at least as many as I have human body cells and maybe a great many more. Eukaryotes, bacteria, archaea – like the different races of humans swarming on the body of the earth, so races of microbiota proliferate on the cornea of my eyes, my mucosa, and along the lumen of my gut. It is a very complex thing to be alive.

'So these star-people,' I press him, 'are they telling us anything? Have they got anything to say?'

'As much as you have to tell them,' he answers cautiously. 'Don't over-invest in the dance of the stars for your guidance, because the Spirit will teach you and lead you into truth, directly. Everything that lives is connected; nothing is separate. Creation inter-is. Where it was straggled and broken, I have healed it, reconciled it, ravelled it up into the Father's love when I offered up my life. I have redeemed it. Within creation there are universes – and galaxies and worlds – and all of them are connected, and they all speak and have meaning. But they are none of them *for* anything.'

'Oh.' This sounds disappointing. 'How can they both mean something and be pointless, purposeless?'

'To be alive,' he says, 'is to breathe with the breath of God. And you don't need lungs for that. It is also true of a plant or a stone. It is called into being by the song of the Spirit. It is God-breathed. And so it has primal purpose – not secondary. It isn't for anything; it is itself. The stars are not for you; they are alive. They have their glory, and it derives only from God. Anything that lives is answerable only to God. Only machines, only gadgets, are made for something else. The stars have their own being, arising from the life of God.'

'So . . . there's nothing to be learned from the stars?' I'm determined to get this clear, and it's proving difficult. 'They aren't saying anything as such?'

'What?' He shoots me that all too familiar quizzical glance. 'Yes, there is. Yes, they are. The stars are ordained by God for times and seasons. Wise men always pay attention to the stars. Because all beings are connected. The truth that is found anywhere is found everywhere.'

As we walk up our front path through the gathering dark, I feel it, what he says. I feel the aliveness and the meaning, the intentionality of life. If I had to put a name to what I sense, I'd call it joy. I'd say it is singing.

13

The magi

*They set out; and there, ahead of them, went the star that
they had seen at its rising, until it stopped over the place
where the child was. When they saw that the star had stopped,
they were overwhelmed with joy. On entering the house,
they saw the child with Mary his mother; and they knelt down
and paid him homage. Then, opening their treasure-chests,
they offered him gifts of gold, frankincense, and myrrh.
And having been warned in a dream not to return to Herod,
they left for their own country by another road.*
(Matthew 2.9-12 NRSVA)

I don't buy many Christmas presents. Turning the feast of
the Incarnation into a massive orgy of consumerism gen-
erating myriads of baubles and worthless trinkets does not
hugely appeal to me. Even so, as we celebrate God's lavish
and unconditional love wrapping around the world in an
outpouring of grace, it seems appropriate to find gifts for
those people in my life who might otherwise feel lonely or
left out, who might feel forgotten.

This is why right now Jesus and I are in the ground floor
of our town's only department store. The perfumery and
jewellery section are always on the ground floor near the
front door, to catch the impulse buyer – and that's where

we are. He's been sniffing all the men's perfumes in happy experimentation, while I've been hovering over a display of sparkly earrings. We meet up near the handbags, and I suggest going up to the café on the top floor to think things through. Getting the right gift for the right person is difficult, isn't it?

We find a table near the window where the beautiful light from the sea floods in, and I contemplate Jesus tucking into a mince pie and a cup of hot chocolate with marshmallows and whipped cream.

'Gold, frankincense and myrrh,' I say to him. 'Not much changes, does it? Choosing gifts that convey how treasured somebody is, how deeply valued. That's the point. Gifts that will mean something to them. Wise men choosing what is fragrant and costly, to communicate how much they cherish and esteem the one to whom they bring their gifts.'

Of all the gifts my life has brought to me, I cannot think of one more special and amazing than having Jesus listen quietly while I turn over the endless ruminations of my heart, exploring deeper, tunnelling down, trying to feel my way to wisdom in my personal experience of reality.

'Travelled in the dark, didn't they? Like we all do,' I go on. 'They made their way by the light of stars that vanish behind clouds, with nothing to guide them but a belief system they practised faithfully. They followed stars and dreams and they stayed close together, and they brought the best of what they had along with them, in the hope that they'd find you one day. And they did. They came to the house where the young child was, it says. What does it mean, Jesus? That wealth acquires meaning when we lay it at your feet, at your disposal? That all truth is God's truth, and every pathway of faith can be the track into your presence? That we should pay attention to the intimations of the natural world and the strong insights of dreams because we are on the trail of mystery? That the best we have is meant to be given away? That we should walk, so far as lies within us, in the path of peace, discreetly avoiding confrontation but refusing to collude with cruelty?

'When I think about them, I can see their eyes shining, dark in dark faces, yet bright with intelligence and understanding. They look back at me down two thousand years, their treasures held in their hands – the treasures of darkness wrapped in the shadows of time, revealed by starlight and imagination. And they fascinate me. But the main feeling I get from them is absolute otherness. I'm not wealthy, I'm not Persian, I'm not a man and I live in the twenty-first century. Who even are they, to me?'

By this time, Jesus has finished his cocoa. I don't know if you knew this, but he is not above wiping his finger round the inside of his mug to get the last bits of marshmallow and cream. Jesus is not proud.

'Living respectfully with difference,' says Jesus, 'is one of the hallmarks of the kingdom. The chased gold vessel of wealth and the hand-carved wooden box of poverty, they each have their own beauty. Life is rich in infinite variety. The secret of joy is to eschew comparison and pursue your own path in faithfulness.'

This Sunday will be our chapel Nativity service. The children have been practising for months. Together they will tell the story over again – some of them dressed in sacks with tea towels on their heads to be shepherds, three of them in the splendid regalia of the magi, Mary in blue and Joseph holding his lantern, one in white with tinsel round her head to be an angel, a little kid in leggings standing on a chair in the pulpit holding high the star, and the toddlers clad in sherpa-fleece to remind us that even sheep get a look in at Christmas. According to how cooperative they are and how capable of remembering their lines, they are allocated each one a part in retelling the story. And I guess it's the same with me. The art of contentment lies in being glad I have a part to play.

'You all done, then?' I say to Jesus. 'Shall we go back down through the giftwrap department and get everything we need?'

I observe, as we do so, that even a resurrection body finds the timing of getting onto an escalator quite tricky.

14

Herod

*But when Herod died, behold, an angel of the Lord appeared
in a dream to Joseph in Egypt, saying, 'Rise, take the child
and his mother, and go to the land of Israel, for those who sought
the child's life are dead.' And he rose and took the child
and his mother, and went to the land of Israel. But when he heard
that Archelaus reigned over Judea in place of his father Herod,
he was afraid to go there, and being warned in a dream
he withdrew to the district of Galilee. And he went and dwelt
in a city called Nazareth, that what was spoken by the prophets
might be fulfilled, 'He shall be called a Nazarene.'*
(Matthew 2.19-23 RSV)

'Let's go for a walk,' says Jesus. What he intends by this, as
I perfectly understand, is 'You ought to get out in the fresh
air more, and you should move more.' It's just that he knows
me well enough to draw me out rather than shove me out.
Obligation is rarely tempting.

I look up at him standing there, waiting, and I say, 'Okay,
then,' and pull on my shoes. When we do this, we go nowhere
in particular, just walk and talk through the park or along
the up and down streets of this hilly town. Today our feet
take us through Silverhill into Bohemia, then down the road
to where Christchurch school sits in its odd little sinkhole.

Coastal towns are given to sudden moments of rocky cliff, and ours is no exception. St Peter's road runs up the end of a place where the land falls away, and, nestled against the bulwark of the small resulting cliff, Christchurch primary school sits, wrapped around by Tower Road and Woodland Vale Road. Jesus and I lean on the railings, watching the children playing playground games in their morning break.

My own grandchildren don't go to school. They are neurologically atypical, and besides, their mother has a profound distrust of institutions. Her preference is for the fundamentals of life – birth and death, working, playing, learning, cooking – to be rooted in the stable earth of home. I once knew a teacher from Christchurch primary school, who laughingly tossed into the conversation, 'Oh yes, Herod, patron saint of schoolchildren,' and there's a gritty little grain of truth in that joke which is not lost on my daughter. Those words come back to me now, as we watch the kiddies bundling around the playground.

'King Herod,' I say to Jesus. 'What was that all about? That dark and terrifying shadow over your life. Like the shadow of a bird of prey blotting out the sun, leaving little scuttling mice frozen in fear at its approach. Herod! For heaven's sake, Jesus! Wasn't it enough to be crucified? What purpose in the divine pattern does King Herod serve? What solitary useful thing can anyone learn from him?'

I love looking at the hands of Jesus. They are extraordinarily full of peace. Even now, at this recollection of the predatory cruelty that menaced his childhood, hunting him with singularly destructive and focused persecution, his hands do not clench or twist. They still rest, loosely linked, as he leans on the playground railing.

'Sometimes,' he says, 'a woman or man of faith must speak truth to power. There are times to give account of the wisdom and authority within you. There are occasions when you are brought face to face with the forces of this world, and you have no other option. These are moments both of courage and of peace because when there are no choices, what else can you do?

'But in general, it is wise to take a path of quietness and lowliness. Avoiding confrontation takes you further. Keeping to the tracks that run close to the hedgerow, the humble, unimportant ways, keeps you out of trouble and extends the scope for loving and for staying alive. Wisdom, like water, flows round the boulders in the stream. Humility is not offended by stepping aside. The word of life is nurtured best by quietness.

'When the time was fulfilled, I came to Herod's palace – Herod Antipas, you know, not Herod the Great who massacred all the babies – and he wanted to see a miracle. He was disappointed.

'It's a blindness, you see? Mistaking the signs of God's presence for party tricks, as that fox Antipas did, or mistaking the signs of the kingdom for political rivalry, like his father. It would be laughable if it were not so bitterly sad. Deluded and suspicious, in their egocentric world, enthralled by Mammon, they cannot see the sweet light of day. They live chained in the dungeons of their own labyrinthine mines, out of the fresh air, stuck in the confines of their own fetid preoccupations.

'I think you can learn from this. In your own life, already, you have encountered the narcissistic and psychotic, the puppets of power and hierarchy, those who are enslaved by their senses and those who cannot find their way back to honest truth. You know how impossible it is to reason with them – wily and mistrustful and jealous, they see an enemy when they look at you, however hard you try. You put out your hand to reassure then, and they sink their teeth into it. What can you do? Avoid them, that's all. When they come looking for you, be somewhere else. Keep out of their clutches. Their path is not yours. You don't need to be in the same place.'

The bell is ringing to call the children in, and it's starting to rain. We move on. As we walk together, Jesus says, 'Possess your soul in peace and keep your own counsel; go your way. But remember: do not permit your spirit to hound them with hatred or blame. Of all people on earth, these prisoners need your compassion. Let them go, and do not follow them; even so, bless them as you part company, with the love of the Lord. After all, you never know. Miracles still happen.'

15

Joseph

This is how the birth of Jesus the Messiah came about:
his mother Mary was pledged to be married to Joseph,
but before they came together, she was found to be pregnant
through the Holy Spirit. Because Joseph her husband
was faithful to the law, and yet did not want to expose her
to public disgrace, he had in mind to divorce her quietly.
But after he had considered this, an angel of the Lord appeared
to him in a dream and said, 'Joseph son of David, do not be afraid
to take Mary home as your wife, because what is conceived in her is
from the Holy Spirit. She will give birth to a son, and you are to give
him the name Jesus, because he will save his people from their sins.'
(Matthew 1.18-21 NIV UK)

'Jesus,' I ask him, 'don't you ever worry?'

'About what?'

He turns his head to look at me, his eyes full of amusement and kindness. I never saw anybody look so relaxed and at home in the world. There's that perspicacity too. When Jesus looks at you, you certainly know you've been seen. 'What is it you're worried about?' he says.

'So many things. Money, my family, work deadlines. How to square all the circles and keep all the balls in the air and spin all the straw into gold.'

'And right now,' he asks me, 'what problems have you got right now?'

'Well . . . I suppose . . . none, really.'

'So it's a habit then, the worrying?'

'Yes. I guess it is. So – you don't ever worry?'

He smiles. 'I learned a lot growing up with Joseph about appropriate responses. He showed me how to fashion a life of peace. For one thing, when God spoke to him, he listened. When Joseph discovered Mary was pregnant, that could have kept him awake at night, couldn't it? He might have fretted about his reputation, or what to do, or just let it gnaw away at him. But he didn't. Instead, he decided the best course of action was to quietly end the relationship – and Joseph did everything quietly. Chatty, he was not. Quiet, decisive, measured, thoughtful. He didn't lie awake worrying; he went to sleep in peace – and then an angel came to him in his dream. When he woke up in the morning, he knew everything between him and Mary was okay, which I'm sure you'll agree was a better result than anxiety would have got him.

'Then after I was born, we were dodging Herod and his family for a long while, moving from place to place until it was safe to settle. I think it's fair to say most people would be worried by the life of a refugee, by having to pick up work where you can and be grateful for charity and help wherever you go. A carpenter likes his own workshop with his things around him. Joseph did have his bag of tools, but he had to make shift without a lot that he really needed. He didn't complain, and because he didn't worry we just saw it was all right. He trusted in God, and it was his job to look after us, and that's what I grew up knowing. Of course, he didn't tell me people were trying to murder me; he kept that to himself. He just moved on, and kept me out of harm's way. He didn't believe in worrying, in borrowing trouble from tomorrow. "Sufficient unto the day is the evil thereof," he used to say.

'Then there was that mix-up in Jerusalem when I was a lad.'

'When they lost you,' I say, 'and searched high and low for you, and eventually tracked you down in the temple?'

'That's right. When they finally found me, my mother – who always had something to say – took me to task. She said they had been worried out of their minds. Joseph didn't say anything.'

'Ha! And you asked them why they'd been looking for you – asked them, didn't they know you would be in your Father's house? I wonder what Joseph made of that. Do you think he found it hurtful?'

'He didn't really understand,' Jesus says, 'but he listened. Then he just took me home. Like I said, he was a quiet man. Quiet, conservative, cautious and methodical. I had something of my mother about me. She wasn't impulsive, but she had the boldness of trust. She was a confident woman. With a strong social conscience. And like I said, she always had something to say.

'I worked alongside Joseph every day. He taught me his craft – Joseph was a very able carpenter. He took good care of his tools, and he was a skilful workman. And one day, not long after they lost me at the Jerusalem festival, while we were working side by side, he remarked in a casual sort of way, "Even if you know everything, sometimes it's better to keep some of it to yourself." And I saw that was so. I remembered it, and I learned the wisdom of silence as well as the imperative of speaking up. I saw it wasn't wise to cast your pearls before swine. I realized it wasn't helpful if people rushed about telling everyone they knew that I had healed them. Silence keeps the way open, where too many words tend to block it.

'Living with Joseph was an education in silence fostering the word. He showed me how quietness nurtures the prophetic spirit, how the word forms and grows under the skilful shaping of silence. The seed develops in silence deep in the earth, waiting for its time.'

'Although silence,' I say, 'can be almighty disapproving.'

'Oh, yes,' he says, 'but Joseph wasn't that kind of man. Some silences are a form of withholding, but his quietness was more about acceptance, and biding his time, and thinking things through, feeling his way into the reality of a situation, putting his hand on truth. Then silence becomes presence.'

I know exactly what he means. 'That's how it feels being with you,' I say. 'So often we don't even speak at all. You are just with me. And in the silence I feel loved and understood.'

'Good,' says Jesus. 'Well, that's how it was with Joseph. He had the quietness of a man at peace with himself. And he knew better than to waste his energy on worrying.'

16

Children and babies

'I am the Lord's servant,' said Mary; 'may it happen to me
as you have said.' And the angel left her.
Soon afterward Mary got ready and hurried off to a town
in the hill country of Judea. She went into Zechariah's house
and greeted Elizabeth. When Elizabeth heard Mary's greeting,
the baby moved within her. Elizabeth was filled with the Holy Spirit
and said in a loud voice, 'You are the most blessed of all women,
and blessed is the child you will bear! Why should this great thing
happen to me, that my Lord's mother comes to visit me?
For as soon as I heard your greeting,
the baby within me jumped with gladness.'
(Luke 1.38-44 GNT)

Jesus is sitting on the floor in my room, peeling a large orange. There's this sense of Christmassy contentment as the beautiful fragrance of it fills the air. I love oranges. I love Christmas. He and I have been wrapping presents, choosing which paper for which person. Then he's been writing the labels and I stuck them on. If you get a Christmas present from me this year, Jesus wrote your name on the label.

It's evening now, and I've drawn the curtain against the blackness of the night. Soon time to light the fire. But during the afternoon when we were out walking, I asked him about that place in Mark's Gospel[2] where people brought children to Jesus wanting him to touch them and bless them, just when he was in the middle of some very interesting teaching about divorce. The disciples tried to intervene and make them wait until the important discussions had finished, but he would have none of it and actually got really cross with his friends. 'Hey! Let the children come to me,' he said. 'Don't try to stop them! They're your actual citizens of heaven's kingdom!' Or something like that.

But Jesus has been to our church and seen the children. And heard them. He's been in a position to observe a small boy wailing loudly in the middle of the service because he's given his face carpet burns flopping up and down like a fish. He's seen them all wriggling along under the chairs in a line giggling wildly when the readings were boring. He was there when the oldest child, who should have known better, gave the whole tribe of them the idea of undoing the (merely decorative) gifts under the tree on the second week of Advent, during the first hymn. He saw the fight that broke out over who got to play with Moses' fibre optic burning bush. People stopping children doing anything is the least of the problems in our church. When you let the children come to Jesus and don't try to stop them, you do have to live with the consequences, is what I wanted to say to him.

But Jesus says that wasn't really what he meant. 'Go on, then,' I say. 'Explain.'

'It's all come a long way from the hills of Galilee,' he says. 'What's under discussion now is reverent conduct in church. It's worth talking about that, but it's not the same thing. Someone coming close to me, and touching me, can happen in a church service, undeniably. But it might not, and it can equally happen anywhere else. If you're looking for me, sooner or later you'll find me, because I'll be looking for you too. We'll find each other wherever you happen to be.

'And the important thing with the children is to respect their agency. In general, they take seriously, and believe, what their parents take seriously and believe. Children know when they encounter something real. They feel the moving of the Holy Spirit. Even a child not yet born knows the presence of God.

'Children don't respond very well to going through the motions. And most of them don't enjoy being paraded as the Young People, made to stand there and sing "Away in a Manger" because it's the children's song.

'Some of them like to join in, to have a go, and some like to watch from the safe place of their mother's side. They don't respond well to rules like Don't Touch, Don't Move, Don't Speak, Sit and Listen, Sit There and Be Good.

'And if in the end, it all amounted to sitting at a table at the back doing colouring, occupying themselves while an adult drones on in the distance, all they've been given is something to leave behind.

'They are a litmus paper for the presence of God, an indicator for how authentic and vital is the encounter. Children have a hunger for what is real.'

I see the sense of this. 'Of course, lots of churches don't have any children in them,' I remark. 'And not everyone who comes to church has children.'

'Every church has children,' Jesus says. 'Everyone has at least one child. To understand how this works, you have to go within. Somewhere inside, you yourself are still a child. What does that child say? What does that child need? Is she allowed to speak, to express agency? What makes her flourish and relax?

'Do you remember that time Zacchaeus climbed a tree to catch a glimpse of me?[3] When I invited myself to his place for tea? The man who came scrambling down full of eager joy, excited at being offered something real, was the child who'd been hiding inside him. Who wanted a chance to join in and had been waiting forever for his turn to come.'

I try to feel my way to what this might mean in practice. 'So, the whole thing needs to be more simple and more childlike? Less segregated and more for everyone?'

'It mainly needs to be honest,' Jesus says.

17

Gifts and graces

I will give you the treasures of darkness
and riches hidden in secret places,
so that you may know that it is I, the Lord,
the God of Israel, who call you by your name . . .
I am the Lord, and there is no other.
I form light and create darkness,
I make weal and create woe;
I the Lord do all these things.
(Isaiah 45.3, 6b-7 NRSVA)

'You sound angry,' says Jesus. 'Are you angry with me?'

I stop, momentarily distracted from my rant. I didn't know being angry with Jesus was an option.

'I'm not exactly angry,' I say, but then I realize he's right, and I am. I mean, Jesus wouldn't be Jesus if he wasn't right, would he?

'It's more that I'm frustrated,' I confess to him, 'by lack of recognition.'

And he waits, as Jesus always does, as I search deep inside to find the words for what I want to tell him.

'I get tired of being invisible and passed over. I get fed up with being belittled and dismissed and ignored,' I say. He knows this well, but still I need to tell him.

'It's not only me,' I go on, 'it's a problem that pervades throughout my family.'

And then I talk to him about the first Sunday we had this Advent, when most of the children from church were somewhere else, and responsibility intended for a whole group of kids, in readings and prayers and lighting advent candles, fell entirely on my grandchildren.

They managed brilliantly, but my heart went out to my grandson. He is ten and has ADHD. It is almost impossible for him to keep still for two seconds together. He grasped that it would be essential for him to actually stay present in the same room as the rest of us, ideally near his allocated chair, so he equipped himself with a wobble cushion and fidget toys from the box we keep at the back of chapel for our neurologically atypical kids.

And he fought with all his might to stay with us. It meant he had to lie flat with his back pressed to the floor, one fidget toy in either hand, pressing and squeezing, his face grimacing. He stayed, and he managed his readings and prayers, and played a full part in what we did. Then as the service ended, he pulled his sweater up over his head, curled up under his chair, and wept from exhaustion. And what do they see, casual bystanders observing our family? A naughty boy who won't sit still? A tall, big lad racing around in church, impulsively hugging his mother and rolling inappropriately on the floor? People cannot see what he brings and how hard he tries. The effort and shining goodwill in his heart is practically invisible.

I tell Jesus about it, and he knows. He was there, and he saw, and he understood it all.

'These are the treasures of darkness,' he says to me, quietly. 'Treasures people don't understand or can't always even see. These are the dark gifts placed into our hands. Like the dark kings from the East, who offered their frankincense and their myrrh. Of what use is rare and arcane incense to a carpenter who can only afford two pigeons for his sacrifice? But they received them, Joseph and Mary. They took the dark, strange gifts into their hands and waited to see what it might mean.

'These children who are born different, who struggle to find their place, they bring dark graces, they are born to a time of darkness, natives of all that is puzzling and hard to understand.

'These are dark times humanity is passing through, but in time, light will dawn. In the end these children of struggle will be seen for who they really are. How much they tried and how dearly they loved will come to light. So much will be realized that wasn't appreciated at first.

'But for now, if they are only given the chance, they can help humanity find a way through the darkness, because theirs are the gifts and graces of darkness. Through habituation, they breathe its air and know its pathways.

'If it helps – I know it might not, but if it helps – everything you give, every part of yourself that you offer in humility and generosity, all the work you put in and how hard you try, I see it. I know it for what it is. I know you do your best. I take into my hands the gold and incense of your offering. I know how costly it is, and how it overflows with meaning. I know you are bringing the choicest wisdom of your heart's love. I do not take it lightly. I receive it and see it for what it is. And perseverance does pay off in the end, but recognition often comes only after it ceases to matter to you. Set it aside. Make your choices according to true and intrinsic value; don't waste energy on longing to be admired.'

There are days – and this is one – when I feel so very, very lucky to spend time with Jesus. There is such inexpressible comfort in his understanding. It's like sitting by the fire on a cold night. It's like a candle flame's quiet brilliance dispelling the shadows. He helps me to see things differently. It's not that anything changes in my exterior circumstances. It's more that his presence illumines the inside of me, the private chambers of my heart, the place where I keep hidden what matters to me as well as where I nurse the wounded places in my soul back to health.

I know that even if nobody else can see it, Jesus takes note of my grandson's courage, bravely doing his best. And under the gaze of Jesus all things are made well.

18

Angels

There were shepherds out in the field, keeping watch over their
flock by night. And an angel of the Lord appeared to them,
and the glory of the Lord shone around them, and they were filled
with fear. And the angel said to them, 'Be not afraid; for behold,
I bring you good news of a great joy which will come
to all the people; for to you is born this day in the city of David
a Saviour, who is Christ the Lord. And this will be a sign for you:
you will find a babe wrapped in swaddling cloths and lying
in a manger.' And suddenly there was with the angel a multitude
of the heavenly host praising God and saying,
'Glory to God in the highest,
and on earth peace among men with whom he is pleased!'
(Luke 2.8-14 RSV)

The penchant for certainty leads us into arid terrain. It encourages the architects of religion to trade mystery for doctrine. This is always reductionist. It is not possible to package or require or trade upon the presence of the Holy Spirit of God.

I stand in the street with Jesus, looking at the department store window's Christmas display. Between the snowy fir trees above the mannequins of laughing children in bobble hats and Nordic sweaters hangs a cardboard cut-out of a herald angel dressed in a long, sparkly frock, a slender golden trumpet raised decoratively to her lips.

'Angel' has become merely a metaphor in our times. When I provided some useful nutritional information to support the health of his son, my friend texted me, 'You are an angel.' I appreciate the compliment, but clearly he's never met one.

It's commonplace to refer to nurses as 'angels', and this has both elevated medical staff to angelic status and reduced real angels to being merely nurses. The pretty lady with luxuriant hair in a white dress, which we are appraising in the department store window is the inevitable outcome of this diminution, the devaluation of *mysterium tremens* into the more easily accessible quotidian banal. An adorable little girl dressed in a sheet with a circlet of tinsel round her head, a Sunday School teacher telling us an angel is a messenger, God's postman, in effect. A fat gilded baby with wings suspended from the roof. And we grow up thinking that's what an angel *is*.

This is a frog-boiling scenario. We swim in its lukewarm waters comfortably unaware, and slowly the life of spiritual power is cooked out of us. 'Angel' becomes merely a synonym for 'a nice person', or useful for the décor of a stately home. Something to hang on the Christmas tree.

'I do know five people who have personally met angels,' I say to Jesus, as we move off down the street. 'One of my daughters saw them blazing in the sky when she was lost and frightened as a little girl. Another of my daughters saw four of them, two either side of the bed where I was giving birth to her little sister. She mistook them for doctors because they were arrayed in white. I had a friend who saw an angel arising as a glorious light when she woke up one morning. Another friend opened the door and found an angel standing outside. It gave her such a fright, she said, 'Please go away,' and shut the door. When she cautiously re-opened it, the vision had departed. And I met a night-club bouncer who was thrown twenty feet through the air in a traffic collision; an angel, again dressed in white, came and knelt at his side as he lay on the tarmac, to see him through. Do they actually wear white, Jesus, or is that just so we will recognize them?'

'They are robed in light,' he says, 'that holds within it every colour of the spectrum. They are the harbingers of wholeness, of shalom. When you see light whole, it looks white to human eyes. The full array of glory is held inside it. It's the original light of the making, the creative Word. That's why they are the angels of God's presence, his emergent breath. When God speaks, his Word comes forth as being – whether that is the Son of God, or the living earth, or an angel of his presence. It depends on the circumstances and the intention of the mind of God. It's how I Am manifests in the world of humans.'

He steps aside to let a posse of shoppers surge past, through the narrow gap between the store fronts and the festive skating rink set up in the retail centre. 'I know what you're thinking,' he says, as we are able to walk side by side again, both of us sparing a glance for a lethally delicious display of chocolates. Jesus does in fact always know what I'm thinking, and I call this an unfair advantage, because I tell you straight, I certainly do not always know what *he's* thinking. 'You think an angel is always glorious – magnificent – awe-inspiring. Don't you? But look, you have to remember the heart of God is love, and God's presence is peace to you. Every angel ever encountered has been the emanation of God's love. That comes in many forms. Doesn't it?'

I have to agree. 'So you're saying in effect,' I concede grudgingly, 'that sometimes the kiddie in the sparkly frock, or the tired nurse at your hospital bedside, can be in fact the actual angel?'

'I'm saying that the different levels of reality are often mingled or superimposed,' he says. 'There is really no such thing as the ordinary. That's how come people can entertain angels unawares.'

He glances at me. 'That's a quote from the Bible,' he says.

I feel a twinge of indignation. 'Yes! I do know! It's in Hebrews.' I can't help sounding defensive, and he grins.

'Just checking,' says Jesus.

19

Homelessness

So let's go outside, where Jesus is, where the action is—
not trying to be privileged insiders, but taking our share
in the abuse of Jesus. This 'insider world' is not our home.
We have our eyes peeled for the City about to come.
Let's take our place outside with Jesus,
no longer pouring out the sacrificial blood of animals
but pouring out sacrificial praises
from our lips to God in Jesus' name.
Make sure you don't take things for granted and go slack
in working for the common good; share what you have with others.
God takes particular pleasure in acts of worship—a different kind
of 'sacrifice'—that take place in kitchen
and workplace and on the streets.
(Hebrews 13.13-16 MSG)

It's nearly the end of the day. The Salvation Army band is playing carols in the town square as the shadows lengthen toward the end of the afternoon. They're collecting money to help the homeless people.

We stand there together, Jesus and I, listening to the mellow sound of brass instruments played by musicians who have been doing this all their lives. The group harmonizes comfortably to make one melded sound – the song of Christmas tradition. It stirs my heart and captivates my soul. I love the Salvation Army band.

And then, 'Everyone is homeless,' Jesus remarks.

'What?' I subject him to one of my incredulous, old-fashioned stares.

'Seriously,' he says. 'Oh come on,' he adds, as I continue to radiate disbelief. 'You know me. I don't deal in glib platitudes. I mean it.'

'Go on, then,' I say, as we push off through the crowded streets, the air still shining with 'Hark the Herald Angels.' 'Explain. One of the chief blessings of my life is the privilege of a warm, dry home, with my own room and a comfy bed to sleep in every night. I walk by these poor souls huddling into their sleeping bags in shop doorways as the evening comes, and humbly thank the Father I'm not required to walk that path. It's a hard road to tread, and I live near enough to the edge to be grateful every day for what I have.'

'Yes,' says Jesus, 'I know. I am there on the streets in the small hours of the morning, when the dew falls and the cold freezes the marrow. I see the shame and the despair of life on the very furthest rim of human margins. But that's the point. Everyone is in exile who walks this earth. The world is beautiful, sure enough. Part of the intention of earthly life is to wonder at the setting sun and the song of a nightingale, at the new moon rising, the freshness of the air and the loveliness of frost. But even so, earth is not your homeland, heaven is. The work of humanity is to see one another safely home. Life's journey is full of glory and miracles, a chance to discover and grow, a place to deepen and strengthen your spirit. But at the end of it, you go home – so your home is not here. Finding the way home is the nature of human endeavour. Everybody here is on the way. What life asks of you is to travel together, to be a kindly lantern and a good companion, to share your food for the journey, the bread of your souls.'

'Like the Salvation Army collecting money to help people who are homeless?'

'Yes,' says Jesus. 'Like that.'

'Travelling home . . .' It's hard to find the words for this. I know what he means, but it fills me with foreboding. 'It terrifies me, Jesus. I'm growing old. I feel like a pilot entrusted with landing a plane where the engines are failing. Somehow I have to bring this thing down safely and gracefully, without crashing into anyone else or ploughing a massive furrow and creating a fireball. The responsibility of managing an ageing body and diminishing income feels immense. My life has passengers, you know? I want to be able to land without hurting anyone else, and I'm not sure – I'm honestly not sure – I have the skill.'

This has always scared me. I first began to think about it when I was expecting my first baby. The point when it sinks in that there is no going back; contemplating the reality that there was me and there was the baby, and the only way out for the baby was through me, and that was going to hurt and take courage. This comes round again now as I grow old, the knowledge that I am trapped inside this complex and disintegrating organism, my exit dependent on material failure of body parts. That won't be comfortable or pleasant, will it? What will happen to me, on my journey home? Will I be blind? Will my teeth fall out? Will I be invaded by cancer or lose my mind? Will I become incontinent? Will my heart split, in one quick and decisive calamity? While I have the time to up my game, what can I do to increase my piloting skills, and manage the landing safely in one piece? How can I ensure a dignified, well-managed landing of this dying craft? What does it take to touch down in peace?

We are walking together, Jesus and I, walking slowly back home up the hill from the sea. I'm tired now. I'm ready to sit down, and I'm longing for a cup of tea.

'Don't forget,' says Jesus, as the sky blushes rose, the setting sun streaking vermilion light across lavender, under the grey billowing of cloud. 'You don't have to do this alone. You have a co-pilot.'

He, who was nailed to the cross and hung there all by himself, surely knows what it means to have somebody to do this with you.

I say to him, 'Thank you, Jesus. Thank you for being there to see me home.'

20

Shepherds

When the angels had left them and gone into heaven,
the shepherds said to one another, 'Let us go now to Bethlehem
and see this thing that has taken place, which the Lord has made
known to us.' So they went with haste and found Mary and Joseph,
and the child lying in the manger. When they saw this, they made
known what had been told them about this child;
and all who heard it were amazed at what the shepherds told them.
But Mary treasured all these words and pondered them
in her heart. The shepherds returned, glorifying and praising God
for all they had heard and seen, as it had been told them.
(Luke 2.15-20 NRSVA)

There's something about the winter night, isn't there? So dark and deep and cold, and it just goes on for so long. It's like falling down a well, or groping blind. It seems to draw your soul right out of its socket, drifting away from its moorings. You lose yourself. It feels like midnight, like two in the morning; it seems to have been night for ever, must surely be time to go to bed now – then you look at the clock and it's something paltry like a quarter past seven. I never want to go anywhere at night in winter, just stay at home by the fire like a bear in its cave, waiting for the spring. And tomorrow is the winter solstice, bearing the weight of the year's longest night. But life goes on and things still have to be done, so I've walked along to the supermarket with Jesus to get some tea bags and cat food – not for the cat, for the seagulls. They stand outside the window on the water butt, our seagull pair, gazing at the food in the kitchen with longing eyes, rapping on the glass with their beaks if we take too long getting theirs. They should be called Scavenger Gulls not Herring Gulls, but my personal conviction is they should be eating fish. So I get them cat food.

I feed the crows and the fox, the badger and the gulls, and the songbirds, and I'm willing to share the kale I grow with the thousands of munching offspring the butterflies leave behind. 'I love this earth and its creatures, and according to my light I do what I can to take care of it,' I say to Jesus, as we stroll along the road home in the darkness. 'Yes,' he says, 'me too. We do it together.'

Taking in the improbable possibility of my small-scale contribution being in any sense part of the work of Jesus, I think of the shepherds on the night he was born, alerted by angels lighting up the night like emergency vehicles, coming down from the hillside to see the saviour of the world.

'They left their sheep,' I say. The great thing about Jesus is you don't need to patiently explain your train of thought. He knows anyway.

'I suppose that was okay,' I continue. 'Sheep can look after themselves for a few hours. Mind you, so can wolves and mountain lions and jackals. Are there jackals in the hills above Bethlehem?'

'Yes,' says Jesus.

'What a night that was,' I ruminate. 'There they were, minding their own business. I expect they had a little fire to sit by, and maybe one of them was playing a pipe to pass the time. Then suddenly the skies opened, and they saw the glory, which is all around us that we can never normally see even though it's always there. And they didn't just say, "Thank you very much, how interesting" – they actually bothered to make the journey to find you. Then afterwards, when they'd seen you, there was nothing else to do but go back up the hill to check on the sheep and carry on where they left off. But it must have changed them, those shepherds, don't you think?'

'I'm entirely sure it did,' says Jesus. 'You know my story of the Prodigal Son?' (Yes, of course I do.) 'It's something like that. You leave home, leave your regular occupation, whatever it may be. You leave behind your flocks and fields or your father's farm, and go in search of the vision that speaks to you or the siren voices that call you. Like the three little pigs who went into the world to seek their fortune. And later you go home. But when you get back, everything is different, not only because life goes on and circumstances change while you're away, but also because you yourself have changed. Finding the courage to leave home and learning the way home again – these are two of the greatest endeavours in life.'

'Also,' I say, 'there's a knock-on effect for the people around you. The prodigal son had an uptight brother who needed to be told he was allowed to have a party. The shepherds must have had partners and friends, and surely they didn't keep what they saw to themselves.'

'Probably not,' says Jesus. 'Though truth is, as they say, stranger than fiction. You can tell people, but they usually don't believe you. It's hard to recognize the unfamiliar. That's what I mean: it takes courage to leave home.'

A thought comes to me. 'You left home too, that night,' I say. 'And what a phenomenal act of trust and vulnerability that was. You came to stay with us, for a while. And when you went back home, you held all the torn threads of human sorrow in your hand, and connected them up again with the broken other ends in the Father's love. You took the whole world back with you, when you went home again. And it hurt you. You came here with nothing in your hands, a defenceless child, and you left your body nailed to a cross at the end. I think of you as changeless, because that's what I've always been taught, but it isn't true. Because when you went home, you had scars.'

'That's right,' says Jesus. 'Every journey changes you. You go home different. But whatever they did to you, and however much you suffered, you do still get to go home in the end. Because I opened the way. That's what I came here to do.'

21

The manger

*For you know that it was not with perishable things such as silver
or gold that you were redeemed from the empty way of life
handed down to you from your ancestors, but with the precious
blood of Christ, a lamb without blemish or defect. He was chosen
before the creation of the world, but was revealed
in these last times for your sake.*
(1 Peter 1.18-20 NIVUK)

[John the Baptist] *saw Jesus coming toward him, and said,
'Behold, the Lamb of God, who takes away the sin of the world!'*
(John 1.29 RSV)

Jesus says, 'Oh, look!' So of course I do. And there's the
sweetest little goldcrest, tiniest bird of all, flittering about
on the bare twigs of our greengage tree, then hopping down
into the hydrangea, finding what insects the wood still har-
bours at this time of year.

You can't make an appointment with a goldcrest. The
very best things this earth affords, you cannot schedule or
buy. You just have to be there, to have time on your hands.
Some of life's most memorable moments are attached to
loose ends. If you tie them all up, you miss so much. It's
important to leave space for happiness to alight.

We watch, rapt, delighting in the minute bird, until at last it speeds away with a whirr of wings, fast and direct as an arrow, and is gone from the garden.

'I know what I meant to ask you yesterday,' I say to Jesus then. 'How did those shepherds know where to find you?' When the angel said the Saviour had been born in the city of David, and they'd find him swaddled and lying in a manger – how did they know where to look? I mean, even then there were several hundred people living in Bethlehem, weren't there?'

'Yes,' says Jesus. 'About three hundred.'

'Right. And loads of extra visitors because of the census – ancestral ties and whatnot. So surely, there must have been loads of stables, all with mangers in them. How come they knew which one? Did the angel go with them and show them the way?'

A frown of slight perplexity momentarily creases the brow of Jesus. 'Well, no,' he says. 'There was only one place to look. You know about the tower at Bethlehem, don't you?'

'No. What tower?'

'Oh, right. Well, Bethlehem was where they reared the lambs of David's flock – the ones for the temple sacrifice. There was nothing casual about it. To fulfil the criteria making the lambs acceptable for sacrifice, the shepherds had to keep the ritual when the lambs were born. At lambing time they brought the ewes down from the hills to the shepherds' tower – Migdal Eder, the Tower of the Flock.[4] To qualify for sacrifice, the lambs had to be without blemish, so when each one was born, it would be checked over to be sure it was perfect. Then, if it passed muster, they'd swaddle it to prevent any possible injury, and temporarily place in the manger.

'So, when the angel told the shepherds they would find the baby wrapped in swaddling cloths and laid in the manger, they knew exactly where to go and look. Migdal Eder is on the road into Bethlehem from Jerusalem, just outside the city. Mary and Joseph would have passed it on their way in. They knew there'd be space and it would be quiet in the tower, because it wasn't time for lambing, it was the mating season – that's why the shepherds were out in the hills with the flock, keeping watch. To separate the mated ewes, as well as protect the sheep from predators. They came down to the valley later, in the winter, when the harvests were gathered and the gleaners had been over the fields. After that, the sheep could have what was left of the wheat stalks, and overwinter in the valley. The lambs would be born in the spring.'

This was all news to me. 'So . . . you weren't born in a stable, then? Why does the Bible say you were?'

'It doesn't,' says Jesus. 'It says I was laid in a manger. It's just that mangers are generally found in stables, so people jump to conclusions, just like they always do.'

I think about this. 'Then, you – it's all part of the story! You were the lamb without blemish. The sacrificial lamb. And your cousin John knew all about that, when he said . . .'

'That's right,' says Jesus. 'That's exactly how it was. And it was the right and duty of those shepherds to inspect the sacrificial lambs. That was their job – making sure the Passover lamb was flawless.'

'Jesus,' I say, 'that's amazing! So, in Judea, the mating season for sheep is December.'

'September,' Jesus corrects me. 'A ewe carries her lamb just shy of a hundred and fifty days. The lambs are born in March, like they are here, when the grass is sprouting green to provide good feed for the ewes.'

'Oh. So are you telling me 25 December isn't your birthday at all? You were born in September?'

'Yes,' says Jesus.

'Then, why . . . '

'The feast of the Incarnation,' says Jesus, 'is about the light of God coming into the world. It's not a birthday party. It's theological.'

'You're going to have to explain that to me,' I tell him, and he promises me he will. 'But maybe save that for another day,' says Jesus.

22

Room at the inn

And it came to pass in those days, that there went out a decree
from Caesar Augustus that all the world should be taxed.
(And this taxing was first made
when Cyrenius was governor of Syria.)
And all went to be taxed, every one into his own city.
And Joseph also went up from Galilee, out of the city of Nazareth,
into Judaea, unto the city of David, which is called Bethlehem,
(because he was of the house and lineage of David) to be taxed
with Mary his espoused wife, being great with child.
And so it was, that, while they were there,
the days were accomplished that she should be delivered.
And she brought forth her firstborn son, and wrapped him
in swaddling clothes, and laid him in a manger;
because there was no room for them in the inn.
(Luke 2.1-7 KJV)

'So, just a minute,' I say to Jesus, my hand poised on the remote control for the TV, 'have I got this straight? Mary and Joseph went to that tower with the difficult name for you to be born?'

'Migdal Eder,' says Jesus. 'The Tower of the Flock. Yes, they did.'

We've just sat down with a cup of tea, lit the fire and switched on the Christmas tree lights – this involves crawling about on the floor squeezed in the gap beside the armchair, to hold down the button so the lights pulse and twinkle calmly rather than flashing on and off like an epileptic strobe – and we're about to watch a repeat we've already seen repeated before, of Pointless.

'So they didn't stay in the stable that belonged to the inn, when the innkeeper said there were no rooms left?'

Jesus looks at me. 'How much do you want to see Pointless? Because none of what you just said happened.'

'What? So what did happen, then? No, I'm not bothered about Pointless. I've already seen this episode twice; I know the right answers, and I can even remember what the wrong answers were. We can watch House of Games later instead. Tell me about Mary and Joseph and the inn.'

'That's the point,' says Jesus. 'There wasn't an inn.'

He takes a sip of his tea, but it's still boiling hot and he almost spills it, so he puts it back down on the table.

'You've got the picture of the kind of man Joseph was? The sort of person who would always do the right thing. He was honourable, and protective – and a man of deep faith. Well, that's how the rest of his family were, too. When the census took place, Mary and Joseph had to go to Bethlehem because that's where Joseph's family came from – you know that, it has it in the Bible. But could you imagine any credible scenario where Joseph would arrive *late* for a census? Or put off travelling when Mary was so near her time? The story is always told that when they got to Bethlehem, all the rooms were fully booked. Joseph, I tell you, was the world's most cautious, prudent and highly organized man. Twice he took me out of the way of murderous kings when I was a baby. Joseph was not a spontaneous individual. He planned. He thought things through. He had connections.

'Not only that, but could you envisage any situation in which a man like Joseph might turn up in the village he came from – where plenty of his relatives still lived – with his wife in the early stages of labour, and none of those relatives would take them in? That couldn't happen, could it? If you think about it.'

'Oh,' I say. 'No, I suppose not. Where did the story come from, then?'

'It's one of those things that got lost in translation,' says Jesus. 'Because they wrote down the gospels in Greek, and then it went into Latin, and then everyone had the King James Bible, which was where the misapprehension crept in. Right there, in Luke's gospel, the King James Bible says Mary laid her baby in a manger, because there was no room for them at the inn.

'The word that's being translated there is *kataluma*, but it doesn't mean "inn". A *kataluma* is a guest bedroom. An inn, a place like a hotel, was called a *pandocheion*. It wasn't so much like a Travelodge and certainly not the Hilton – just a dormitory to sleep in and a refectory to get a evening meal. But that's where people passing through would have stayed.

'So when Joseph took Mary to his relatives' home, they were welcomed – *of course* they were. They went in and had a nice meal and enjoyed catching up on family news. But then it became clear that a few twinges earlier in the day were developing into the real thing. Baby on the way. There isn't room in most people's *kataluma* for everything you need to have a baby – mainly, other women to help you, and somewhere to put the baby, and things for washing you, and a lamp stand. The *kataluma* had enough space for Mary and Joseph to tuck in together for a few nights, and space to snuggle a baby in between them. But you need more room than that to actually give birth. And that was when one of the women spoke up and suggested the Tower of the Flock – because it was all set up for giving birth, and only just down the road, and not used at that time of year.'

'Set up for giving birth?' I gape at him. 'Yeah, but . . . sheep?'

Jesus shakes his head. 'These weren't just any sheep, remember? These were the lambs without blemish. The shepherds took better care of those ewes than most people did their own wives. She was right. It *was* the perfect place.'

'So Mary, poor thing, had to trudge half a mile down the road while she was in labour?'

'That helps sometimes,' says Jesus. 'Giving birth isn't an illness.'

He tries another cautious sip of his tea, and it's cool enough to drink. I turn on the telly.

'I'm going to remember all that,' I tell him. 'You never know; it might be on Pointless one day. A *kataluma* is a guest bedroom, and the word for what we call an inn now is a *pantechnicon.*'

'Almost,' says Jesus. '*Pandocheion.*'

23

Mary

'Blessed is she who believed that there would be a fulfilment
of what was spoken to her from the Lord.' And Mary said,
'My soul magnifies the Lord,
and my spirit rejoices in God my Saviour,
for he has regarded the low estate of his handmaiden.
For behold, henceforth all generations will call me blessed;
for he who is mighty has done great things for me,
and holy is his name.
And his mercy is on those who fear him
from generation to generation.
He has shown strength with his arm,
he has scattered the proud in the imagination of their hearts,
he has put down the mighty from their thrones,
and exalted those of low degree;
he has filled the hungry with good things,
and the rich he has sent empty away.
He has helped his servant Israel,
in remembrance of his mercy,
as he spoke to our fathers,
to Abraham and to his posterity for ever.'
(Luke 1.45-55 RSV)

I don't really like this. The day is closing, the sun has gone off the rim of the horizon, the sky is in any case heavy with swollen dark clouds, and the trees on either side of the path serve only to intensify the shadows. This is only our park, but all sorts of people come here. As night falls, I think it extremely likely the people I wouldn't mind meeting will have gone home for their tea, while others I'd prefer to never encounter will start to gather. Like the weasels in the Wild Wood. Feral.

I don't like being here all by myself. I sing 'Abide with me' under my breath. Then I begin quietly whispering a prayer – 'For thou art with me . . . thou art with me . . . though I walk through the valley of death . . . thou art with me . . .'

'Hello,' says a familiar voice. 'Are you okay? Were you looking for me?'

And, yes, I'm okay now that I can see for sure that Jesus is with me. He flashes me a reassuring grin, and we walk along together.

'Your mother,' I say, 'was one intrepid woman.'

'She was,' agrees Jesus.

'It's not as if your part of the world struggled for want of crooks and robbers. Look at that story you told about the road to Jericho – the man who fell among thieves. Look at Herod, slaughtering kiddies right and left. Look at Jephthah, hiding out in the hills with a posse of bandits. And there's Mary, fresh from her encounter with an archangel, striding up into the hills all on her own to see her Auntie Elizabeth.'

'Cousin,' says Jesus. 'But that doesn't take away from your point. And yes, not much gets between my mother and what she intends to do. Even now, actually. She brings her influence to bear on the way things are. She is still full of grace, and the Lord is still with her. People who try to mess with my mother are wasting their time. She wins the day.'

'I form the impression,' I tell him, 'that she was a very political person. Like she would take the fight to the foe and not be cowering out of sight. She cared about the plight of the poor and the oppressed. Mary's expectation and intention were that we should get off our backsides and make a difference. She strikes me as a woman who was not afraid.'

'That's right,' says Jesus. 'She saw the world through a very clear and distinct lens, my mother. She had very pronounced moral values. And it was her conviction that we should always do what we can to help. Spin straw into gold, change water into wine – my mother is both fearless and optimistic.'

'Did it shape you,' I ask him, 'her worldview? Is it fair to say you are Mary's son as well as the Son of God?'

He considers this. 'I see her in myself,' he says. 'I learned from her. Our lives, you might say, grew entwined around each other, like the twisting stems of ivy climbing a tree. But, you know, that's also true of everyone who makes common cause with me. You become part of heaven, as much as heaven becomes part of you. You become part of what makes divine being complete. Like a jigsaw puzzle.'

I take in this information. If he hadn't said it to me himself, I'd have discarded the notion as presumptuous – that who and what I am could add anything to the shalom of God.

'It flows,' Jesus says. 'God's grace flows into and through the world like blood through veins. It flows and it grows, developing organically, feeding and sustaining and bringing love to birth.'

'Like a placenta?' I try not to sound sarcastic, but, 'Yes, exactly like that,' says Jesus. 'The Spirit of God enfolds the purpose of your growing soul like a nurturing womb. And you in your turn are called into the world as a Christ-bearer, a light-bearer. The living earth shines with the radiance, the *shekinah* of God, and it grows within you, until you become as full of eternal life as a wave is full of the sea.'

In the time we've been talking, we have climbed the steep alley leading to the steps, which come out on the road where I live. I realize that, my mind full of what Jesus is saying, I have completely forgotten to be afraid of the lonely, dark places. I must remember this. Presumably it can always be so.

24

Be here now

He was in the world, and the world was made by him,
and the world knew him not. He came unto his own,
and his own received him not. But as many as received him,
to them gave he power to become the sons of God, even to them
that believe on his name: which were born, not of blood,
nor of the will of the flesh, nor of the will of man, but of God.
And the Word was made flesh, and dwelt among us,
(and we beheld his glory, the glory as of the only begotten
of the Father,) full of grace and truth.
(John 1.10-14 KJV)

Christmas begins, for me, with the BBC broadcast of carols from Kings College, Cambridge. But the thing is, there's more than one version. Every Christmas Eve it's transmitted on BBC1 on the telly, in a form carefully chosen and modified for popular tastes in the modern world. Meanwhile, on BBC Radio 4, you can hear the original, traditional version, with the bidding prayer that emerged from the travail and sorrow of the First World War, 'let it be our care and delight to hear again the message of the angels, and in heart and mind . . . go even unto Bethlehem.'

As if the heart-stopping beauty of the original form of words were not enough, there's another tradition to the annual ceremony of carols at Kings. The service always commences with 'Once in Royal David's City', the first verse sung unaccompanied by the solo treble voice of one of the young choristers, a child. In preparation for this very special act of worship, all the choristers learn and practice the song. Silence descends on the medieval chapel, and you can hear on the radio the faint susurration of many people gathered, all waiting quietly together, invisibly transmitted along the airways like the Communion of the Saints. None of the choristers knows which of them will be singing the opening solo until the moment comes, and the choirmaster points to the one he has chosen. Everyone must be ready, but only one will sing. The choristers say it is at the same time terrifying and an honour you treasure all your life.

I make up the fire and boil the kettle for a cup of tea. I draw the curtains against the day that is already navy blue. I sit down beside Jesus on our battered old sofa, and make sure we're tuned in to Radio 4, then mute the sound until it's time for it to begin.

I suppose the ministry of Jesus must have started in something like the same way. He grew up in Nazareth, son of Mary, learning carpentry from Joseph, the first of a straggle of brothers and sisters, playing with the other boys from his village.

Like every Jewish child he observed the Law and the Sabbath, he heard the scriptures and memorized the psalm chants and learned about the longed-for Messiah, who would come one day to set his people free.

What was the moment, I wonder, when he saw the finger pointing steadily at him? When did the *kairos* come in which life whispered, 'Now!'? Was he afraid as he stepped forward into his destiny? Did it help to know himself as the chosen one?

I ask him, 'Whatever was it like?'

On this holy night, when he came into the silence of a waiting world, among the stars and the shadows, the first-born child of the girl who gave her *fiat* to the angel, what did he know, Jesus the light of the world?

Jesus, blowing reflectively on his tea as he always does, says, 'It was the same for me as it is for everyone. There are the terrors and agonies of whatever we are called to, the things we think we will never get through. And perhaps we do not entirely. Life leaves us scarred. It is our scars that become the badge of who we are, even when we rise again. But each one has her task to undertake; each one has his place in life that makes the pattern complete. We anchor the light wherever we are, too close to see the unfolding of the pattern. We do our best. We respond to God's call on our lives.'

"We?" I say. 'You identify yourself with us? With ordinary, blind, struggling humanity?'

'Well, yes,' says Jesus. 'That's what I came to do. I wanted you to know that whatever life throws at you, I am there with you. When you sob, crushed, in the midnight hour of your Gethsemane, I am there. When you lie helpless as they hammer in the nails, I am there. When you surrender to the strong muscular spasms of childbirth, I am there inside you and with you, bringing my light into the world through your patience and courage. I am *involved* in humanity – and humanity is involved in me. I am with you; that's what it means to be me. You can find me in whatever place you find yourself. In a prison cell, in a funeral parlour, at the work-bench of a factory, walking along the road where you live. I am there. I am with you.'

And yes, here he is, sitting on our distinctly shabby sofa in the living room of this semi-detached Victorian house in East Sussex. It's true. He is here.

Jesus nudges me and nods at the clock. 'I think it's starting,' he says. 'I think this is it.'

I lean forward to unmute the speakers on my laptop. And it's time once more to bring every power of our heart and soul to wait upon the uplifting of the voice of this little lad, who holds the melody for hope to make a new beginning.

25

The infant light

In him was life, and the life was the light of men.
The light shines in the darkness,
and the darkness has not overcome it.
There was a man sent from God, whose name was John.
He came for testimony, to bear witness to the light,
that all might believe through him. He was not the light,
but came to bear witness to the light.
The true light that enlightens every man was coming
into the world. He was in the world, and the world was made
through him, yet the world knew him not.
(John 1.1-10 RSV)

It's very dark.

I wake early, usually about four o'clock. It's a time of day I love in any season of the year. I rest in the silence. I listen to the dawn chorus. I watch the sun rise.

But today, at four o'clock it's still completely dark. If I pull my curtain back a little, I can see the stars.

When I say *completely* dark, I should qualify that. We live in an urban street, and our neighbours have small children. Right outside our house there's a street lamp, glaring relentlessly from dusk until dawn. At the back, the lights from our neighbours' home shines in all night – I think they leave on the landing lights for the kiddies, or something. Two doors down, fearful of break-ins, Dave the builder has security lights on his shed. This means all our gardens are lit up like Wembley Stadium every time a fox jumps over the fence. Our houses back onto the park, which means this happens often. So the darkness is there, but hiding behind a variety of artificial lights.

Inside my room, since Jesus spotted those rechargeable LED candles, I've been able to have a perpetual light on my shrine. It's just a shelf in my bedroom, with a picture of Jesus, and now a light to remind him never to forget me. He says he couldn't possibly, even if he wanted to.

It's so early, not even the buses have started up in the depot. I quite like them actually; their engines hit the exact same bass rumble as a recording of Tibetan Buddhist monks chanting I once heard. So when they turn the key in the ignition around five o'clock, in my imagination it trans-poses to the dawn meditation watch in a Himalayan temple. Brings me peace.

Just now, though, silence. And behind the constancy of artificial light in the modern world, real darkness.

But this is a holy time. This is the hour of the infant light. The old Norse word for Christmas, *Yul*, means 'the Turn'. As the seasons follow their circle, and the earth turns, there comes a moment when everything begins again – and that moment is now.

In everything that is, they say, lies the seed of its oppo-site. The shrivelled, dead old fruit that falls into the ground and rots holds the secret and the blueprint of new life. The deepest, darkest night of the year is the quiet place where the infant light is born. Here, behind the darkness, hides real light.

And this is the moment when the cosmic Christ, the supreme being holding all reality within itself that the Pythagoreans called the Monad, the Logos of God through which the breath of the Spirit sang the universe into life, slipped into the world from the womb of a Jewish girl in one time and place, became a baby, a simple human, like you and me.

This has implications. The work of Christ is all about reconnection – what is shattered, he makes one; what is wounded begins to granulate under his touch; the alienation of heaven and earth is bridged by the new and living way effected by his death and his rising; those who were enemies and strangers become kindred. God was in Christ reconciling all things to himself.

But on this particular morning, it is the moment of incarnation that radiates its quiet and specific light. He has come to us. He is born in us and from us and among us. This is the time of Emmanuel, God *with* us.

For every human being that ever was, there come days of terrible darkness. Times of failure, terror, shame, loss, misery, pain and loneliness. There will be times when inside the chamber of your soul, it will be completely dark, when the light of hope goes out, and you have nothing.

In such moments, it is tempting to cover up the darkness with artificial light. To fill the night with extremes of wattage in a desperate attempt to pretend the darkness isn't there. And I have to tell you, because I have been there, this doesn't work.

When the light goes out inside your spirit, when you fall into the dark night of the soul, try to realize the place you have landed is just before four o'clock on Christmas morning. This is Yul. This is the moment the infant light is born. There, just behind the darkness, waits real light.

'That's why,' Jesus said to me, 'the feast of the Incarnation is set at the darkest time of the year. Nothing to do with my birthday. It's because into the most barren place of the human spirit, where everything is cold and dead and all light is gone, my love comes and finds you. But please, will you notice one thing? This salvation I bring, the light that comes into the world's dark night, is not a rescuer – not a knight in shining armour or a hero with a solution. It's a baby.

'Everybody knows what babies need. Complete 24-hour care. This is the way – and it is the only way – the world can be saved. By drawing forth the love that is already inside you. Not by helping you, but by needing you. That's the way the miracle is accomplished.'

The love of Jesus, it turns out, is drawn forth from you. God knew what he was doing when he sent a baby to redeem the world.

A prayer

Jesus, saviour of the world, I believe in you.
Humbly, I ask you to be the Lord of my life.
I need your love.
Please, Lord Jesus, will you walk with me?
Speak to me in the ordinary things of every day.
Teach me to see the radiance of the Holy Spirit
    in my home
    in my town
    in my family
    in my church
    in my job.
Dear Jesus, I want so much to know you for myself.
I open my heart to you.
Come to my heart, Lord Jesus,
And make it your home.

Amen.

Notes

1 The Greek verb for 'made his dwelling' is *skenoo*, which means to pitch a tent, to make the improvisational shelter for a temporary stay.
2 Mark 10.13-16
3 Luke 19.1-10
4 See Micah 4.8 (KJV)

Notes

WE HAVE A VISION OF A WORLD IN WHICH EVERYONE IS TRANSFORMED BY CHRISTIAN KNOWLEDGE

As well as being an award-winning publisher, SPCK is the oldest Anglican mission agency in the world.

Our mission is to lead the way in creating books and resources that help everyone to make sense of faith.

Will you partner with us to put good books into the hands of prisoners, great assemblies in front of schoolchildren and reach out to people who have not yet been touched by the Christian faith?

To donate, please visit www.spckpublishing.co.uk/donate or call our friendly fundraising team on 020 7592 3900.